CW01022788

Disclaimer and Copyright

Disclaimer - Neither the publisher nor the author is engaged in rendering professional advice or services to the individual reader. The ideas, procedures, and suggestions contained in this book are not intended as a substitute for consulting with your physician or lawyer. All matters regarding your health require medical supervision. Neither the author nor the publisher shall be liable or responsible for any loss or damage allegedly arising from any information or suggestion in this book.

"HAPPY DIVORCE" is also available in E-BOOK form, and in the translated and localised German Edition under the title: "GLÜCKLICH *TROTZ* SCHEIDUNG". Please check: www.rossanacondoleo.com

ROSSANA CONDOLEO

HAPPY
DIVORCE

How To Turn Your Divorce
Into The most Brilliant
And Rewarding
Opportunity Of Your Life!

The Life Changing, Empowering, Most Complete
Guide for Dealing with Divorce

CONTENTS

To my daughter Camilla Johanna Teresa,

for shining in my life

like the morning sun

INTRODUCTION

I have grown old with a strong sense of truthfulness. This applies to my life, to my beliefs, to my projects, to my relationships. Truthfulness must also stay at the base of every marriage.

I really believe in the words *"for better or for worse, for richer, for poorer, in sickness and in health, to love and to cherish; from this day forward until death do us part,"* and with my book, I am not rejecting this institution at all. Nonetheless, as I had to experience myself, there is nothing you *share* that belongs to you entirely; a good marriage cannot be one person's responsibility only. I am convinced that until both partners are committed to their marriage success, divorce will rarely be an issue, notwithstanding the changes two spouses undergo in a lifetime.

My mission is to make sure that those who had neither the chance nor the fortune to sustain their marriage until *"death do them part"* have at least the chance and fortune to live the rest of their lives upon the best possible premise: it was no Happy Marriage, but it will definitely be a *Happy Divorce*! You have the right to be happy, and no one and nothing can bring you so much trouble that you forget who you are and where you want to go. Therefore, I have undertaken to turn your divorce into the most brilliant and rewarding opportunity of your life! In this aim, I wrote this complete, all-around guide, which will be explaining, enlightening, advising, answering, highlighting, focusing, supporting, motivating, helping, developing, improving, guiding, calming (short meditation and visualization practices, as long as positive affirmations are also included), empowering, and energizing you through and after divorce.

Part I is more spiritual, preparing you and setting up the basis for later approaches and responses to the more practical subjects contained in the second part. You will learn to:

ϡ manage the stress of divorce;

ϡ discover and observe your mental abilities and the power of thoughts under a number of different theories (scientific, religious, common sense);

❧ shift your energy to meet the physical demands of having to cope with divorce;

❧ lighten the emotional burden that accompanies this event;

❧ ease your frustration;

❧ regain your sense of control over your life;

❧ discover new possibilities;

❧ become aware of the paradoxical inner power triggered by divorce (which otherwise would be disrupting since this event is second only to the death of a spouse on the Stress Scale) and use it at your advantage;

❧ contact your inner Self to learn what you really want and what your *original* dreams and goals are;

❧ set goals in every sphere of your life; and

❧ motivate yourself to start your life projects.

Part II addresses sensitive/critical issues you are generally confronted with while facing divorce in connection with:

❧ job

- ❧ family

- ❧ friends

- ❧ appearance

- ❧ home

- ❧ health and fitness

- ❧ ex husband/wife and their people

- ❧ social networks

- ❧ public image

- ❧ back into dating

- ❧ children

- ❧ divorce lawyers.

The assimilation of information, concepts, ideas, and self-help solutions contained in this book will positively permeate your new life from the very beginning of your reading. You will straightaway feel comforted, corroborated, stronger, and authentically self-reliant, so that problems will no longer be central in your life. Finding happiness and fulfilling your dreams will become the protagonists of your thoughts. And this will happen as a natural but amazingly fast maturing process, with no particular effort; you are just required to believe in my words and in your ability to arrive wherever you want. Anything you acquire is mostly the result of your own initiative and engagement. Yet, feeling happy and achieving the first wished results will provide you with the optimism and energy needed to turn every new challenge into a thrilling possibility.

Happy Divorce will lovingly coach you through and after divorce, remaining a lifelong whispering companion in case you forget how important you are and how beautiful living your dreams can be.

And now, since you might really not want to waste your time reading introductions, we will get into the core and start working on your personal development right now.

Just let me wish you a fortunate, harmonious, successful...

Happy Divorce!

PART ONE

"I See My Way"

I Manage My Mind · I Find My Self · I Set My Goals

COMING TO TERMS WITH DIVORCE - ACCEPTANCE

Acceptance of what has happened is the first step to overcoming the consequences of any misfortune.

- William James (1842 – 1910)

American psychologist and philosopher

Are you just thinking of divorcing, but the chances of a "safe," manageable split are near zero? Are you waiting for that last triggering "enough is enough" (i.e., he or she must behave so badly that Alien is a pale, perfumed doll in comparison) so that it is eventually easier to make the final decision? Both many-year-pondered and bolt-from-the-blue divorces can have the same destabilizing impact on your life. Parting from the ex-loved one is sometimes a real tragedy, especially if you are the weaker party (the one who earns less, who takes care of the children, who comes from a foreign country, and so on). Nonetheless, limbo, or the state of indefinitely postponing an undesirable but necessary decision, can be even more hurtful and devastating in the long run than divorce itself.

Whether you are thinking about divorcing or you are already in the process, the fact is that if you are reading my book, the simplest, most obvious reason is that your marriage does not work! Whether it is your partner's fault, yours, or the circumstances', the relationship with your ex (I will use "ex" as a way of exemplification) has suffered so much that perhaps it can no longer be healed. This turns out to be particularly true if you have already taken all the necessary steps to save your holy union, but any and all have failed miserably (for example, family counseling, vacations and activities meant to regain togetherness, and so on).

Then, as a matter of fact, you have to accept it: accept that notwithstanding any positive effort to change the picture, your marriage is lacking essential elements that make it a happy one. **Acceptance is a very soothing feeling. It releases long-lasting tensions and sets energies free for managing the psychological and physical demands of coping with divorce.** Accepting the end of

most people out there. Please believe me, there are a lot of happily married couples whose sex is great after twenty years together and who care for each other.

Please do not believe that your marriage was a "good marriage" just because apparently (again) your everyday routine worked. And please do not argue that no marriage is perfect! That is the soup some parents have served to their children, mostly daughters, for centuries in order to lower their expectations while hunting high and low for a spouse. A bad marriage was once a lot better than no marriage at all, and I believe that still today, surely in many cultures and subcultures, this concept continues to produce people who are resigned to being unhappy for a lifetime.

What happened behind the curtains at your place? Or what did not happen behind the curtains at your place? You must be true to yourself while reading this book, since digging in the past and recalling painful and frustrating feelings is not at all my job here. What about your real wants, your need for closeness and time together? My experience, and that of many divorced people, is that the first thing lacking when a marriage shipwrecks is closeness. Body and soul intimacy. An entanglement that brings two to become a single unit. And it is visible! I can tell you by observing couples at parties (which is the best milieu to rate relationship behaviors) whether they will resist wear and tear or not.

I am not pro-divorce. I am in favor of the traditional family model made up of the original father plus the original mother plus the original children. This is the model we have grown up with, which *is imprinted in our DNA, and anything different is perceived as disturbing, unconventional, or cheap.* That is totally wrong. The so-called patchwork families have proved not only to be effective in providing care and love to every member, but also to be stronger, through facing daily problems, than traditional families. It is a paradox, but it is true! Indeed, inside other partnering and parenting configurations, such as gay families, for example, people are more flexible, more open, and faster in meeting new challenges. The result is that change and adaptation are the norm, and the extra efforts needed to keep up with more complex family systems are abundantly paid back and rewarded by the goodwill and engagement of all people involved. We would expect the traditional family to be the pillar of society—and it really was, up to forty years ago. But starting in the sixties, Western society's structure changed in its core, so that the enlarged strong and backing family model has been replaced by the stand-alone family, which later transforms, lets partners go away and come in, and generates new children while accepting and loving those already existing, no matter from whom they come from. I may tell you about a lot of working examples of this kind; but you just need to look around, and you will find plenty of them.

Human beings respond at present to more natural rhythms than they did under the rigid and archaic mentality of past times; like falling leaves, dead partnerships must be replaced. If you find the concept is unacceptable and perhaps also a bit immoral (I feel uncomfortable too with this statement—*forever* should be *forever*!), think of how everything in nature is regulated by and follows cycles in order to ensure the continuation of life. These can be different from organism to organism, but it always happens that when something is no longer meaningful for the existence of the others, it simply ceases to exist.

We are warm-blooded animals, and lack of closeness makes us depressed and unhappy. We need love and the warmth we receive from it. In most cases the descent to the bottom of a marriage has been going on for such a long time that nobody noticed it, in that changes for the worse were minimal but steady and continuous. Some literally lose control over their lives because, while suffering in silence (not to bother family and children with marital problems) and trying hard to adjust themselves to every new upcoming unpleasant situation created by the partner, they forget they have a life too and the right to be happy. Others pursue together a rescue plan (mostly for their children's sake, although this may be totally against their own sake!); in so doing, they might succeed in keeping their lives together but may be still unhappy and may be overwhelmed by too many compromises—up to the point at which they feel annihilated, so deprived of their energies and interests and motivation that they simply die inside...day by day!

Now, you are really lucky because this is not your case: you are divorcing! This is the starting point of your new career as a Happy, Divorced Person (from now on "HDP").

I still remember my grandma's hazel eyes as she glanced at the ice-blue eyes of my eighty-five-year-old grandpa across the table during big family gatherings. They were naughty, playful, and timid at the same time, like those of a fourteen-year-old girl. There was pride inside, love, and the picture of the handsome young man who gave her six children and cared for her late diabetes wounds up to her last breath. I really missed this kind of glance between my ex and me, and I waited too long for it to come back. I had to come to the bitter conclusion that when love disappears from one's lover's eyes, it is the same as when life abandons a body and its eyes. This is not a nice connection, but it really conveys the idea of no return! Accepting it is the best favor you can do for yourself and for your children, if any.

You must archive your marriage, since you are now a soon-to-be HDP. What was sick or dead has been cut away. This is a fabulous time for rebirth, and next year you can celebrate the first birthday of one of the richest years in your life, when so many different and wonderful changes took place, making your life plain and happy.

I am here to remind you what you are worthy of and how much power gurgles inside you, just waiting to be unleashed. **You are beautiful, interesting, and just—and you are going to take the biscuit of life, not the crumbs.** There is a whole world of possibilities out there.

Accept the end. Do not fight against it. **Let a healing calmness flow inside you.**

Mini Visualization Practice to Regain Control Over Your Thoughts

1. *Wherever you are, take three long deep breaths: inhale, count to five, and exhale.*

2. *Then visualize the problems connected with divorce as they dematerialize into a small, smoky ball swirling around your head. It is a malicious elf who knocks at your head to disturb your inner peace.*

3. *You are a fairy/wizard, and by winking twice you make the smoky ball simply whirl out of your head (you may need to close your eyes to better visualize it) and disappear. You are now calmed down.*

Repeat this mini visualization practice every time you feel overwhelmed by negative thoughts. The more you repeat it, the more you will master it and obtain the desired results. Also in those situations when your sanity is put to the test, take one minute for yourself and practice this again to regain control of your thoughts and actions.

I do not expect that in doing so, you will forget your divorce, especially if there are still open issues such as financial assessments or pending litigations (about children's custody, for example) and you are required to actively fight for your rights. Give vent to your anger, sorrow, concern, or loneliness, but never indulge in these feelings. Positive feelings attract positive happenings, while negativity attracts negativity, even when you are on the righteous side. There are days that are worse than others, when you wake up with a mourning feeling. But remember that everything comes to an end. I have always been a fan of Scarlett O'Hara (the protagonist of the epic movie *Gone with the Wind*); every time her life came to a blind alley, she would say, "After all, tomorrow is another day."

In order to start a virtual cycle, you first need to accept the end of your marriage and of an age. Acceptance is really the foundation on which you will build your new life and your new age. It can be simply your inner life, or it can extend to your life in general, depending on the number and degree of changes you need to carry out to reach out a fulfilled existence.

Acceptance has a calming, soothing effect, and you need tranquility now to be dedicated to your goals. You will see in the next chapters how to get this tranquility by optimizing every aspect of your life! Have faith in yourself—you are becoming an HDP!

DREAMS AND GOALS

Believe Big. The size of your success is determined by the size of your belief. Think little goals and expect little achievements. Think big goals and win big success.

- David J. Schwartz (1927 - 1987)

Bestselling author, professor, and life strategist

There is a widespread tendency to set goals based on actual—i.e., available—resources. Most people have coped with limitations, either psychological or financial, all their life long. They minimize their dreams so that they become more reachable. This is at least what they think. The bigger the goals, the bigger the outcome, so conversely smaller goals turn out to be smaller in reality!

You must set goals that are in line with your dreams, no matter how big, instead of putting limitations on your creativity and fantasies. Are you willing to move into a breathtaking, ten-room, terraced, ocean-view villa? Then why reduce this wonderful villa to a two-room apartment with a narrow little balcony? Dream of your villa! Think of it as much as you want. Stick pictures of what it should look like, or of similar ones, everywhere at your place, so that you can see and visualize it and anchor this life goal into your subconscious. And the same goes for your income and your future partner, whom you expect to be perfect (at least he or she fulfills 99.99 percent of your requirements), and any other dream you have. You must believe it. **No one can tell you what you have to dream and how far or big you can think**. Do not be ashamed of wishing apparently impossible things! There are only you and I here! If you want to be reserved about your dreams and tell no one, not even your closest friend, do not do it! Thoughts are yours, and dreams are yours, and goals are yours. That's it!

Human beings, like other earth creatures in smaller or bigger form, have been gifted with an enormous power of imagination. Imagination is the ability to visualize and internally experience our creative thoughts. And what happens by doing that? Our brain starts functioning as if the things, the people, or the situations we are imagining were real. Researchers have found that the human brain releases similar types and amounts of chemical substances (endorphins, for example, which are very important neurotransmitters) both by performing certain activities and by just imagining them. Experiments and tests have been carried out also on professional swimmers; they have been asked to stop any physical training during the experiment. They started instead to regularly perform mental swimming training, in which they had to imagine and visualize the whole thing without being able to move. Not only did their brain react emotionally as if really under swimming training conditions, but it also sent to the muscles the same neural inputs as if actually swimming, which resulted in a relevant growth of muscular mass. Amazing, isn't it?

Then, besides taking advantage of the creative positive effects of imagination fulfilling our emotional and spiritual demands, it seems we control it also to get other very interesting results. Mind conditioning is no longer a mere subject of speculation inside the so-called paranormal sciences or treated like Secret Service paranoia, but has gained the respectability and authority of empirical scientific evidence.

Coming back to our field of interest and applying the concept to your personal development, we will be using mind conditioning to stay focused and achieve goals. *"In absence of clearly defined goals, we become strangely loyal to performing daily acts of trivia."* - Unknown Source.

Soon you will be acquainted with *The Questionnaire*. Through simply formulated questions, you will access your dreams, organize them, and start taking action in order to realize (or *manifest)* them. It is no kind of magic. Think about many rich or influential people of the last one hundred years. The majority came from modest families with a low level of education. Andrew Carnegie was the son of a weaver and cotton farmer; Albert Einstein was one of the poorest students in his school, and some teachers thought he could be retarded, i.e., handicapped. Their dreams were so strong that they often kept them awake the whole night—something that all people strongly committed to achieving their dreams share. And the same happens to me! It is a wonderful, creative, very exciting feeling—a waterfall of ideas, at times very structured and organized, at others under the form of positive impulses pretending to be fast converted into action. Under these illuminated circumstances, I obtained my most rewarding results. Some ideas were so innovative, and I carried out so much brilliant work, that I asked myself how I could exude such hot stuff. It is indeed a pretty automatic process that happens when you leave your imagination free to dream and perform. And I know now better than ever (after experiencing a subjugating marriage that terminated with divorce) that when you put aside your dreams to follow and back someone else's dreams (in my case, my ex-husband's), you lose your own life energy. Like a flower without water, sooner or later this becomes apparent, and some consequences can heavily bother you for a lifetime if you do not correct the situation.

I feel alive and happy only when I let my imagination perform and let my dreams free. I then realize that I am a force of nature, and that I can reach whatever objective I want. I will help you to do the same.

Your desire to rediscover your life must burn inside you to generate results, sometimes astounding, very fast results. And **when you believe in yourself and your dreams, everything is attainable.**

Yesterday I watched on TV a documentary about a young man named Kyle Maynard. He is a wrestling champion, a personal coach, and a successful author, and he has lately conquered

Mount Kilimanjaro. None of that is strange—except that he lacks arms and legs due to congenital amputation.

No excuses or hindrances can prevent you from starting to get the life you want! I can tell from my own experience that it is not difficult to switch from a divorce burnout to the life of your dreams, the job of your dreams, the relationship of your dreams, etc. Just the fact of putting yourself into action produces positive changes. *"Inaction breeds doubt and fear. Action breeds confidence and courage. If you want to conquer fear, do not sit home and think about it. Go out and get busy."* - Dale Carnegie, 1888-1955.

Delaying and Postponing? No Go!

Once you have acknowledged that setting goals has nothing to do with your actual, present resources and possibilities, you are now completely free to **start questioning yourself about your true wants**. It would appear to be a kid's game, but it is not. Most people have been molded by parents, school, religion, and workplace to think and act as *it is required and expected*. The result is a growing burden of obligations and duties, which make our wants go behind the first line, then behind the second line, and finally disappear.

Many psychosomatic illnesses and burnouts are plaguing people from every region of the world, just because we allow ourselves to be manipulated—not only by our families, schools, partners, and work environments, but also by consumer industries and their advertising. We must be perfect. We must multitask and be available twenty-four hours a day, and we must have a good social aura so that no one can criticize us. And our bodies must be trained as well (for men a six-pack and for women a C-cup are mandatory), and children must be offered this and that, and learn and perform music, two sports, two foreign languages, etc. We are restlessness. We feel pressure, and we strive for a status that is not aligned with our natural rhythms and requirements (especially in the workplace) and that is above anything that is humanly possible. Most behaviors are imposed from others, little responding to our inner wishes and desires. We accept lifestyles, structures and frames, and models that have nothing to do with our own nature. This is simply VIOLENCE! We are consciously and unconsciously overly abused daily. Too fast a life/work/social pace tires the nerves and body; we are born human and not supernatural or android. Stress kills more people than smoke in the so-called civilized countries.

Living far from our true selves creates emotional instability, less conviction in what we pursue, and mild to very serious nervous disorders (depression, phobias, social deviations, suicidal tendencies, etc.). On the other hand, our biological mechanisms are constantly under fire, so a growing number of health disorders can be attributed to stress and depression, making psychosomatic medicine one of the brightest fields in medical science.

Hectic activity gives most people a false measure of their place and importance in the world: the more they get busy, the more they think they are doing great. If your agenda is full from Monday morning till Sunday evening, you might want to start asking yourself: Why do you not get busy with yourself? Why do you always need to spin around? Are you afraid to be alone? What about having a couple of minutes of pure solitude and letting your soul talk? It can have a lot of interesting things to say! We have different levels of awareness, which come from different levels of consciousness. So although something may seem incoherent, we can judge it in two different manners, depending on the voice we listen to: the one from our subconscious, or the Self, which is linked to our basic needs, survival instincts, body functions, and the fulfillment of our true needs; or the other voice coming from our conscious, which has registered everything that has happened in our life and speaks in terms of experience. When we do not try to harmonize these two voices, then comes a conflict, and unhappiness results. Was your ex-partner really a choice of yours? Or did he or she just embody a model that was good, but not for you?

I do not know if you came to the same conclusion, but I think most people, most of the time, keep their "selves" secluded, locked inside a black cellar, without nourishment and love.

You must now go downstairs and open that door in order to establish successful goals. You must go down and let your Self out and be free to define and organize the life it has always dreamed of. Failing this, you will probably be making the same mistakes—all over again—with any new partner you will be with.

You cannot be happy in a relationship if you are not happy alone. Children's education, your job, your hobbies, your relationships with colleagues and friends, all have to respond to your Self, not to the ideologies you have been nourished with from your very first day on earth. For example, you might discover that you need to be friends to a different kind of people than those you are going to the bar with right now. They are perhaps very far from your usual field of interest (you are a bookkeeper, for example, and you normally go out with colleagues from your consulting company, with whom you always talk about football and taxes). It can be exciting getting to know someone in the entertainment field who invites you to the Concert Music Hall for the premiere of *Orlando*. *Change* is a topical word. By changing habits and usual behaviors, we can experience and learn not only lessons and happenings, but the rest of our new selves. Until we remain confined in our usual world, with same frames, same interests, and same friends, we never know how nice and rewarding something different can be.

I like to stick to the rules. I find structure is necessary to keep complexities together and to better organize them. But rules and structures are guidelines, not confined spaces. So that what we perceive as an "I must do" situation could be eventually revised or replaced by an "I like to do" situation. **When you love what you do in all life sectors, nothing excluded, everything goes smoother and easier, and happiness is no longer an abstract concept or something you get in minutes and beats. Happiness is a permanent feeling and belongs to all those who are in touch with their "selves." It is a simple, basic concept.**

In the next chapter you will be asked, through the Questionnaire, to get in touch with your Self. If you want, you can first read it and then plan the right time and place where you can work.

Take this moment with joy, since you are coming closer to your true goals and enriching your awareness. Again, I know many people who do not let tranquility enter their sphere. They always have consumer electronics in the background, they listen to radio or TV news while having breakfast or taking a shower, and they stay on the phone all the time, even when they play sports. These people are really afraid of silence. Perhaps they are afraid to query their Selves. They do not give themselves time for meditation, or ponder about spiritual phenomena. These people are locked inside a shell, and their Selves are not in a cellar, but a lot deeper.

I hope you are not afraid of yourself or of what can happen when you discover that the order on which you have based your life is not that perfect, or stable, or credible, or reliable, or true to your goals. Your divorce may have challenged this order, too. And now you need to positively address your Self and query it about wills and wants. I strongly believe that this discovery work is the most extraordinary part in your self-development process.

UNVEILING YOUR ORIGINAL SELF AND GOALS

Somewhere along the line of development we discover what we really are, and then we make our real decision for which we are responsible.

Make that decision primarily for yourself because you can never really live anyone else's life, not even your own child's.

- Eleanor Roosevelt (1884 - 1962)

First lady, writer, and humanitarian

We are changing all life long. For better or worse, we change. This is a fact. Most of the cells in our body, including those in our brain, change. Old ones die, and brand-new ones replace them. This is why we can say that the muscles and the bones we have now are not the ones we had five years ago. This renovation process continues until death; it only becomes slower as we get older.

Consequently, when I say "Original Self" or "Original Dreams," I do not visualize you back in your teens pondering what you will do as an adult. By "Original Self" and "Dreams," I mean the Self and the Dreams that have been peeled down to the core, which are naked and raw. This is very important. And yet, you might finally find out that your aims are unchanged since high school. Anyway, please do not look into the past to find answers that you can only find *in the here and now*.

Therefore, we are going to find out what you really want, what your dreams are, your goals, your expectations, visions, and desires. You will be focusing your emotions because through emotions you get a direct contact to your subconscious, to your very Self. The feeling you get in answering the Questionnaire is very important in assessing how true they are. If you feel happy giving those answers, if you shiver just thinking about "What if...," if your heart beats faster, then it was your Self answering. And this is exactly what we want. Please give yourself time to ponder any answer that triggered none of the above reactions. This is also a way to learn how to recognize when you are happy and how to enlarge this feeling until it covers your entire twenty-four-hour life.

Happiness is the positive energy produced by your Self while achieving your dreams. A person deprived of his or her dreams soon becomes unhappy.

Happy Divorce!

PREPARING TO ANSWER THE QUESTIONNAIRE

Success depends upon previous preparation, and without such preparation there is sure to be failure.

- Confucius (551 - 479 B.C.)

Teacher, philosopher, writer, politician

The Questionnaire is an important preliminary step since you cannot set goals if those goals are based on false assumptions or requirements set forth by third parties.

By proceeding with order and structure, you will be able to economize your resources, particularly at this point in your life when you require lot of them to cope with the stress of divorce.

My mission is to help you not only to overcome these challenges, but also to possibly become happier than ever. You will be soon a HDP—take it for granted!

Preliminary Conditions

Before "contacting" your inner Self through the Questionnaire, you need to find a peaceful, pleasant, and silent environment. The first time calculate about two hours or more, since the list of questions is pretty long and encompasses all of your life sectors. Later on, you can repeat the Questionnaire, or part of it, whenever you want, but you will certainly need less time.

Create an appointment on your agenda as you would with any other important things to do. It is for your health/life. It is undelayable. It is necessary.

The place: I would not recommend a street place (like a bar, a square, or a public garden), or any other open, crowded place where you strongly feel the influence of hectic activity and civilization. I cannot expect that you should be able to find an isolated piece of paradise, but should you have a nice, comfortable couch at home, or if you can sit under a tree in an open, natural setting (with grass and/or trees all over, no disturbing noises, no kids, no partners, no friends, only you), it would be perfect.

As I previously said, this act of writing down your dreams is a very important aspect of your personal development. In answering the Questionnaire, you may want to adjust or make changes, and this is normal if not desirable, because it is in line with the process of getting closer and closer to your Self. **Remember that nothing that you will think and write down must be considered foolish, childish, ridiculous, absurd, or unachievable.**

In the aim of turning divorce into the best opportunity of your life, you have to conquer a new level of awareness first and make little preliminary changes in your attitude, which is essential also for coping with the heaviest and most painful aspects of your divorce. You are literally preparing the way for a beautiful new life, the one you have always desired—not the one in which you had to meet the expectations of people, authorities, and institutions. You have to go to the roots and realize whether, for example, you really like and want to be a well-paid financial analyst, or if you express yourself best when dealing with nature. You must assess whether you want to repeat the same mistakes in the future and maybe find a partner who is similar to your ex, or if you need another kind of person beside you, just to list a couple of examples.

What You Need

1. A secluded place, at home or within nature

2. Two hours, at least, the first time you do it

3. No disturbances—switch your telephone off, and be sure your kids or whoever do not come back home before you are finished

4. White paper, A4, not less than fifteen sheets

5. Two pens (one for backup)

Short Meditation Practice

Sit now comfortably.

There is only you there. No one can hear or watch what you think and do.

Relax and focus on your breath.

At first you inhale, count to five, and then exhale.

Repeat this deep, long breath ten times. Stay focused on it. Do you breathe with your belly or with your breast? Or maybe with both?

Now let your breath slowly take its natural pace and read the following loud and slowly:

Affirmations

I feel good because this is my time, and nobody can take it away.

Nobody can make me angry or keep my tranquility away.

I am determined to sensually savor and enjoy life.

Suffering no longer belongs in my life.

I am important, I am beautiful, and I deserve the best.

The world is full of happy and realized people who love and are loved in turn, who earn their money doing the jobs they love, who live in the places they love most, who have lovely friends, children, parents, and partners who support them instead of taking their life energy away. I will be one of these happy and fulfilled people within a very short time.

I deserve more than this, and this more is out there waiting for me.

I just have to wish my dreams to come true, and they will indeed manifest.

I will list my dreams, and this list will exactly mirror my wishes.

This list comes from me and not from my parents, or my superior, or my best friend.

(Only for parents) I will write down my wishes compatible with my responsibilities and duties as a parent, and my nourishing and educating obligations in their respects.

This is my time and my space, and I have a world of possibilities before me.

I avoid thoughts and answers that would cause third persons to be damaged.

I will pursue my interests without being detrimental to other people.

I have only good thoughts and feelings because only good feelings generate good results.

My dreams are possible only if they bring good to me as well as to the people around me.

Setting my goals, I will never forget to remain just and fair.

ROSSANA CONDOLEO

THE QUESTIONNAIRE

The will to win, the desire to succeed, the urge to reach your full potential... these are the keys that will unlock the door to personal excellence.

- Confucius (551 - 479 B.C.)

Teacher, philosopher, writer, politician

Now write down your desires regarding your financial situation.

- ✆ **To be happy, do you need more money than you already have?**

- ✆ **What amount of money would not only solve your present financial problems, if any, but also make you a fulfilled HDP?** Feel how nice the sensation is of possessing so much money.

๑ **How many things could you do and buy with this money?** Do not limit your fantasy, and make a list.

๑ **How many people could improve their own condition just because you become wealthier (maybe your parents, your children, your friends, the Red Cross, or the animal shelter)?** Donating makes people as happy as receiving, and if you receive more, you would like to donate more. Revise the amount above and add some money for generosity's sake.

๑ **Please think about the subject of this section and add anything that comes to mind and makes you feel happy even when you only think about it:**

Now write down your desires regarding your home.

- ❧ **Are you happy in your present home?**

- ❧ **Does this home fulfill the requirements of place, room, and beauty you have always dreamed of?**

- ❧ **Is a town, village, or farm your ideal place to live, or would you rather move to a farm, village, or town?**

- ❧ **Is your ideal home in the mountains or by the sea or waterfront?**

- ❧ **Is it an apartment, or a house with a garden?**

- ❧ **Can you close your eyes and imagine, and then write down, specifically, what would it be like according to your needs and vision?**

- ❧ **Please think about the subject of this section and add anything that comes to mind and makes you feel happy even when you only think about it:**

Now write down your desires regarding your job

- ❧ Is your present work, if any, what you have always dreamed of?

- ❧ Do you wake up every morning eager to go to work, or would you rather take ten cold showers?

- ❧ Maybe you like your job very much, but it is not at the right company, or under the right boss, or with the right colleagues. What would you change in this respect?

- ❧ Is your job in line with your principles, or does it somehow go against them (abortion practitioner, for example)?

- ❧ People are natural beings, like flowers, trees, and animals, and when forced to endure inappropriate work conditions, body and soul damages might result. Think of your work conditions: are you content with them, or are there aspects that have to be improved or changed? For example, is it routine and/or

alienating, requiring more fantasy or freedom? Or is it, for example, too heavy, with more human natural rhythms required?

♿ **Do you not have a job at present? It may be because:**

1. **You are wealthy enough not to need one.**

2. **You have raised your children till now**. But you might now need one as a result of getting divorced. Besides allowing you to earn money, a job can open a whole set of new possibilities in front of you, such as meeting new friends, having new love encounters, and keeping your mind positively and productively occupied.

3. **You still haven't found one.** If you've been unsuccessfully looking, ask yourself if what you write in your CV and the jobs you are applying for are aligned. No matching qualifications? Would you like to do something different? Or do you usually apply for jobs you do not like? Let me explain with examples: you presume you want that job, but in reality you apply only because society, your family, or your ex would expect you to perform such a job. Or you have a degree in art history, and you apply for a job at the

local library as director. It is a very respectable job, the pay is good, and the workplace isn't hectic. It would be a real balm now in your life, and it would solve a number of problems. But you would be alone, or almost alone, the whole time, and the variety of tasks in this role is very narrow—BORING! Notwithstanding an apparently brilliant job interview, your application is rejected. Is that such a surprise? You must have signaled the whole time that you were not interested!

~*~

Please remember that there are many different rewarding and creative ways to earn money; your knowledge base and your competencies might shine best as a freelance professional rather than as an employee, for example.

Another important thing to keep in mind is that if you do not actually possess the qualifications to apply for the job of your dreams, you can go back to school or attend training courses anytime to learn those new competencies. *You can really get whatever you want, provided you really want it!*

ॐ **How do you spend your free time?** A number of people have transformed their hobbies into very attractive and lucrative careers.

- **Write down a list of your dream jobs, those you find beautiful and rewarding in terms of self-fulfillment.**

- **Now give yourself the time to narrow down the list above, and then write down what you would like best to do for a job.**

- **Please think about the subject of this section and add anything that comes to mind and makes you feel happy even when you only think about it:**

Now write down your desires regarding your family.

Family (including father, mother, and siblings; <u>we will deal with children, if any, separately</u>) play a role in attaining your HDP grade. How positive, negative, dominant, or subtle this role is depends on physical distance, family history, the frequency of your contacts, and a lot of more or less important variables. A very large number of choices and actions that have to do with the very basic structure of our lives can be influenced, also subconsciously, from our family background. For example, your choice of a partner for life might have had a lot to do with your parents; i.e., in line with their expectations (to please them), or totally against their expectations (to upset them). It is not always so, of course. Anyway, a good percentage of divorces have to do with partners who could be and were ideal spouses—for Mom and Dad!

✎ **Do you want your father, your mother, and your siblings (if any) to be supportive but not overwhelming?**

Try to understand why you have not succeeded in delimiting your own area. No one can finally bring you to do things you do not want to unless you allow it. You can always opt out, anytime, by phone calls, meetings, etc.

- ✷ **Do you want, on the contrary, them to participate in your life more?** Did you do everything necessary to keep your contacts alive with your family, or were you the one who put distance in the relationship?

- ✷ **Do you want your father, your mother, and your siblings (if any) to be healthier than they are?**

- ✷ **Write down what you would like your relationship with your family members to be.**

- ✷ **Now write down what your attitude should ideally be in that respect, even if you think you will never be able to change it to that point.**

Think of what makes you happier. Measure your happiness while thinking, for example, of "more openness, more love" or "less contact, more independence." Do not think of what would be "right." I do not agree with the saying "You get what you give" because I find injustice exists, although sometimes it might be true. It is very difficult to weigh how much responsibility you have in a relationship. A part of it is formed through interactions that in time produce fixed patterns. This exercise is meant to let your wants come to surface, not to make you disappointed. Should you feel uneasy with this or other topics, just go ahead and come back to the point when you are able to complete your task without painful feelings.

✎ **Please think about the subject of this section and add anything that comes to mind and makes you feel happy even when you only think about it:**

Now write down your desires regarding your children.

If you don't have children, you can skip this section, but I advise you not to. I would like you to take notice of your inner wishes with respect to the future, not the past. Children may also come with a new spouse.

When we undergo divorce proceedings, children are even more a central element in our life, both because we are concerned about their future and because we have to grant them continuous care and love, even when we feel miserable and drained.

- **What would you like your relationship with your children to be?**

- **What kind of qualities should children have to make their parents happy and proud?**

- **Now focus on your children individually, and considering and respecting their own personalities and needs, answer the above questions again.**

You may have prejudices or fears about parenting, or even about the possibility of becoming a parent. If you already have children, you may want to focus on the events, small and big, that made their eyes look bright and joyful. Too often, children react lukewarmly to what we expected to make them glad. Astonishment and disillusionment may follow. So it happens that a little girl may be happier eating an ice cream or playing with stickers than flying to Paris and looking at the panorama from the Eiffel Tower. Considering that adults and children, and also that adults and adults (should your children be already grown up) may have different tastes and expectations and visions than you...

❧ **Write down what a parent is meant to do, in your children's eyes, in order to be perceived as a good father or mother.** This level of understanding is important when our happiness also depends on other people's feedback—in this particular important case, our children.

❧ **What are the things that make you smile when you think of your children?** Would you say you are in a position to foster the possibilities that would make you smile like that even more in the future?

ॐ **Please think about the subject of this section and add anything that comes to mind and makes you feel happy even when you only think about it:**

Now write down your desires regarding your appearance and your health.

Since I cannot see you, I also cannot be of any help in establishing whether you need to pimp your appearance or not. I deem this topic so important that I have dedicated an entire chapter of this book to it. Every coach in the world would tell you that no matter how good you look outside, what is important is how good you feel inside.

And this is true—but not completely. Unfortunately, there are objective obstacles linked to appearance, which makes success in the job and social arena more difficult for those who do not take care of their appearance. Your appearance is something you have to keep always under control because it can continuously change for the worse and for the better. We have to take advantage of this to keep the pointer in the latter direction. For example: in January you have a model body. Then due to an accident, you must stop training for six months. In June you have put on so much weight that in your best friend's wedding pictures, you barely recognize yourself. Then you start a diet plan and go to the gym again. Christmas dinner is no problem; you are again so fit that you can eat for three.

- 👁 **Think whether you should lose or gain weight in order to have a "normal" appearance. Be creative and visualize yourself vividly wearing the size of your dreams. List your target weight and your target size.**

- 👁 **How sporty should you be? This is not really important to me, but you may want your chest to look more masculine if you are a "he" or your hips to look rounder should you be a "she." Just joking!** You can leave it blank if fitness is not your thing. A mild sporting activity can help you keep yourself healthier, though!

- 👁 **Visualize yourself with the appearance of your dreams and write down your description, excluding things you cannot change (such as stature, skin color, or physical handicaps) and including any other details (hair, skin, hands, teeth, etc.).**

Bad habits should be absolutely left behind, and **I would advise you, straightaway, to make a resolution to give up smoking or**

drinking or using drugs, should you be dragged under by addictions.

Good things happen, even under the most unfavorable circumstances. Paradoxically, now is really the time to make great big changes, and this involves also thoroughly cleaning your body of any substances that might have left it unable to react to adverse or life-changing circumstances.

❧ **If you are an addict, write down your desire to quit (smoking, drinking, taking drugs, or whatever else).**

While you're coping with a bad marriage and then with divorce, the energies at balance can end up in the minus field. More stress for the body and the mind can bring divorcing people to overreact to any subsequent situations, and this is a vicious circle that has catastrophic side effects on your life and on your general health. Acid reflux, heart rhythm disorders, insomnia, fibromyalgia, panic attacks, fatigue, and MCS (multiple chemical sensitivity) are only a few common examples.

❧ **If you are suffering from one or more psychosomatic disorders, write down in your wish list that you want to get rid**

of them and become a stressless, healthy, poised person.

Everything is possible, not only for people from reality TV shows or best selling success stories or magazines. Everything is possible for you too. **Starting to make wishes is the very first stone for building your dreams.**

How long ago did you receive your last compliment about your clothing? Like, "Oh, you look gorgeous in those jeans/skirt/jacket..." etc. If you do not remember when, then it might be time to...

❧ Express a desire to wear something "stylish."

If you argue that substance is important, and that you have to work at your substance alone to feel better, you are not at all wrong. Nonetheless, you have to think about the part of yourself which, more or less consciously, receives, absorbs, and reacts to the influence of people's opinions. And let me say that there are really a few among us who really do not care what others think of us. In some way, we are always positively or negatively influenced by people's feedback during our interactions. And the most sensitive of you are also the most vulnerable. This might, for example, be because you close yourself in a shell and avoid social contacts since you do not like to see how "the others" jeopardize the image you have of yourself. And you must also admit that there can be something true in the way the others perceive you, especially when many people in different contexts perceive you in the same way. Sometimes we must simply face it: there is a dichotomy in how we think we are and how we really are.

Improving oneself aesthetically may turn out to be much more rewarding than simply addressing your inner qualities and your social competencies. **It makes you a lot more self-assertive and confident.** This is crucial and really matters when you have to defend your rights (against your ex-spouse, for example) or look for a job or attend school meetings, etc. Looking good—and **by looking good I do not mean "beautiful" but well groomed**—greatly improves your chances of being socially successful. Divorce can have such dramatic consequences for some people that they simply stop taking care of themselves. I hope you are not and will not be among these people.

- ❧ **Please think about the subject of this section and add anything that comes to mind and makes you feel happy even when you only think about it:**

Now write down your desires regarding your divorce.

Stay and remain positive and fair; you do not have to take revenge for anything. He or she used to be your better half, although now he or she might be behaving like a jerk and driving you crazy. So try to mitigate the "horrors" of dealing with lawyers, assessments, your fear of losing your children, or house, or money, or whatever, and think only about the positive things you can obtain from divorcing—but not more than it is fair for you to obtain; this is very important. You are not going to feel good later on if you try to take advantage of the other party's weaknesses or if you challenge your ex with unethical requests and expectations. Now you no longer have your ex-spouse interfering with your choices—for example, any choice from adopting a pet to moving to a new town you like. Or it can be that you now can read in bed or play Nintendo all night long!

❧ **You have the chance to give plenty of room to your creativity here. Open your heart to a world of possibilities. List everything that comes to mind and** makes you smile and rejoice—such as "I want my divorce to be over soon!" for example.

Now write down your desires regarding your ex-spouse.

How it used to be before and during your marriage is history. In this section, you are required to be realistic in formulating your desires and goals. If, for example, your spouse already has a new partner sharing not only their life and home but also their own children, it is worthless for you to wish that he or she would come back to you. Reconnecting with a "dead" love is psychic's job, not ours.

~ **Write down any positive wishes you may have that you know will improve your actual situation between you and your ex.**

If you find it unbearable, for example, to deal personally with him or her, you can just wish for more physical distance between you. If he or she is trying to make you appear a jerk in order to obtain sole custody of your children, then please do not wish him or her to die of cancer (which would be natural, but not the best here!) but to be enlightened or better guided.

There are so many divorce constellations, and the reactions of two ex-spouses dealing with each other can be so different! Settling every dispute can help a lot to clarify the sky. Until then, the two are often just opponents engaged in a fight. How cruel it can be mostly depends on the lawyers who defend them, and secondly on their native characters. So take a long breath because every nightmare ends with morning sun.

❧ **Please think about the subject of this section and add anything that comes to mind and makes you feel happy even when you only think about it:**

Now write down your desires regarding your future partner for life.

Perhaps you have divorced because you moved or want to start a new life with your new partner. Or you are freshly separated or divorced and had the luck to quickly find your twin soul. In these cases you can obviously skip this section.

If you are going through a period of detoxification and perceive any representative of the opposite sex (it can be the same sex for gays) as a serious threat for you and your future plans, it is OK. You can be really happy alone, because when you stay alone, you know exactly where you are and where you are going. Breathing this sense of freedom brings oxygen to your life. Again, it is OK. We both know, though, that the time will come, sooner or later, when you trust the other sex again and you will be willing to share your new sofa with a special someone.

Not every man or woman is a clone of your ex-spouse. Otherwise there would not be so many happily married people over there, or people sharing their whole lives together, becoming old together, and still holding hands while walking in the park. Never give up the hope of finding your soul mate. We are making plans for the future!

Ehm...let me say two more words. Perhaps you have come to the idea that your partner for life must not necessarily be your perfect match. You might have been told to be practical, since the quest for your ideal partner can turn out to be lifelong. You might have come also to the conclusion that you need to adapt and compromise because people who look unattractive (always under your personal scale, not as an absolute value) can be wonderful parents and mates in turn. Open your ears and listen to the following words: **These are only clichés!** The truth is that there is no particular law that tells you how a person really is, or if that person is good for you, based on his or her outer shell. This is the reason why you can ask to meet the partner of your dreams—and this means the whole package.

- **Describe him or her in detail and give a precise "form" to your wishes.** You will visualize the object of your dreams and feel his or her presence by you every day until he or she will really appear in your life. Believe it or not, it will happen! Complement descriptions with personal qualities. I am just giving you a few hints. Think as if you were literally ordering your future mate right now. I am sure you will enjoy it!

- ❧ **How should your future partner look?**

- ❧ **What sort of character should he or she have?**

- ❧ **How would you like him or her to relate to you?**

- ❧ **How would you like to relate to him or her?**

- ❧ **What kind of qualities do you expect him or her to display at home, at work, and with children?**

- ❧ **Should he or she be able to grant you financial security?**

- ❧ **What age should your future mate be, more or less?**

- ❧ **What would you like him or her to do for a living?**

If this is not important to you, leave it blank. There are some professions, though, that are very "peculiar," and people prefer to have partners with similar work backgrounds. Think of actors or people working in the entertainment industry. The fact that they often get married to one another is not just the product of chance. They can simply better understand and support each other when it comes to having no regular income, long absences, or unforeseeable career breakdowns.

Without trying to influence the choice of your future partner, I completely agree with a prospective lover who has my own tastes, or similar ones, and with whom I can share common or similar objectives. It is tiresome, in the long run, having to adjust any and all aspects of your being to someone who is completely different. It can be amazingly refreshing and interesting to meet someone very different from you. But then you spend more time thinking about how to fill the gaps and avoiding disputes rather than enjoying your time together. Modern rhythms do not allow families and couples to use their time in any other way than constructively, in love and peace with one another. Anyway, it is you here who has to set goals. Smile!

✎ **Please think about the subject of this section and add anything that comes to mind and makes you feel happy even when you only think about it:**

Now write down your desires regarding any other things in life that are important to you and that you may want to change or improve.

- ✑ **If you are not content with something important to you at the moment, something very topical for your self-fulfillment and inner balance, you must think about how you want these things to improve. Write them down and imagine the rosiest outcome.**

- ✑ **Think about hobbies, travels, further education, or whatever your heart desires.**

- ✑ **Please think about the subject of this section and add anything that comes to mind and makes you feel happy even when you only think about it:**

~*~

When you are finished with the Questionnaire, you may feel really tired, or excited, or both. By writing down your desires, you have achieved a precious new awareness.

You now possess a brighter view and awareness of your original goals and are no longer at a starting point. You are already on the way to self-improvement.

YOUR POWER OF CREATION

We are formed and molded by our thoughts. Those whose minds are shaped by selfless thoughts give joy when they speak or act. Joy follows them like a shadow that never leaves them.

- Gautama Buddha (ca 563 - ca 483 BC)

Philosopher, spiritual teacher, and founder of Buddhism

~ * ~

Each man must look to himself to teach him the meaning of life. It is not something discovered: it is something molded

- Antoine de Saint-Exupéry (1900 - 1944)

Renowned novelist, poet, aviator

There are a lot of different thought movements and currents and sources, both from the past and from the present, declaring how important it is to know what you want, to state it clearly, and decisively pursue your objectives. Decisively means determined and consistent. And determination is first of all a state of mind.

You are looking to graduate as a Happy, Divorced Person (HDP), and you will succeed too, no matter how complicated your life is right now, no matter how much grief you have accumulated, no matter what your financial means are right now, and also no matter if you suffer from any form of addiction right now (which may be the result of the bad relationship with your ex and all the consequences connected therewith). You are stronger than all of that, stronger than you think, believe me. You have been made perfect. You have the power to overcome any and all obstacles and defeat any and all opponents. You will not only be a survivor after that, but a real conqueror.

People possessing nothing but their dreams have reached the highest peaks of success in any field. They all had something in common: they believed in their dreams. The most famous and broadly known is: *"I have a dream"* from a speech by Martin Luther King Jr. on August 28, 1963. We also know what kind of mountains his dream moved, what the dream of a single person meant and achieved for all of mankind.

Now, you have a very important and precious list in front of your eyes. The list of your dreams!

I guess you have not paid much attention to the layout while answering the Questionnaire. It can look chaotic and disorderly. Therefore, I ask you to organize and compact the answers into a new document so that it looks nice and easy to read. A great idea is also to make a *motivation / action* or so called *vision board* out of it by aggregating images that help visualize your words. For example, if you have written that you want to earn more money, you can write down the amount and paste a picture of many bank notes or a picture of you tearing up a copy of your mortgage (signifying that you have already paid the balance). You could complement the dream about your home (if any) by pasting a picture of one that looks very much like the one you would like to buy or build. You can find on the Internet tons of non-copyrighted pictures that you are allowed to download and print for private use.

It is important you hang your *vision board* (you decide the size) in a visible place so that you can see it easily. The best spot could be at your workplace near or above your desk; alternately, if you are private about your dreams and goals (which is sometimes preferable), put it anyplace at home where it can be frequently seen.

You should be able to read the list of your dreams at least once a day—before going to bed is the best time because during the night your subconscious will work at it. On the other hand, you should not be annoyed by this repetition. You can just create the image of your document or vision board in your mind and recall it once or twice a day. Thoughts are a lot faster than eyes, and visualizing your vision board (with closed or open eyes) instead of reading it works in the same way. You will discover little by little what a tool you have at hand, provided it really corresponds to your true desires.

The Art of Timing

A deadline is generally essential to setting goals. You can indeed give yourself a deadline for all of your wishes and write them at the top. Example: *By March 15, next year, I want to go on vacation to the Maldives with my new partner for life.* Too long a time line can sometimes be demotivating. Your target lies so far away that you hardly can see and hit it. Too short a time line can be upsetting; sometimes you just need more time than planned to get to your goals. You would rather stay vague about deadlines and think and express your desires in such terms: *"As soon as possible, I want to go on vacation to the Maldives with my new partner for life."* Visualize yourself sipping a colored drink at one of those beautiful palafittes on the transparent waters of the Indian Ocean. Your HDP plan can be really funny. You can think of your dreams wherever you are, at any moment of the day, and just by visualizing them, you program your mind and subconscious to act in the direction of their fulfillment.

Awareness and Drive: Through Different Disciplines into Mind, Subconscious, Imagination, Thoughts, and Their Molding Power

My aim in this section is to give hints, to open or broaden your mind on certain topics, to let you think over and beyond what you may have learned as truths. Then you will be able to use your new awareness very much like a vehicle that takes you exactly where you want.

I have asked you to do some things and to think in a certain way, which is meant to turn you into a Happy, Divorced Person. Now, how this happens can be more or less interesting for you. You can be a perfect driver without knowing how an electronic ignition works! This is the reason why I do not make a scientific treatise out of this chapter and invite readers who want to learn more to independently explore further the issues that arouse their interest.

The mechanism that brings us to the finish line has multiple, converging explanations. Most of them have scientific value and have been empirically validated.

According to most successful people, reaching goals involves a combination of focus, determination, and luck. It seems that luck (meant as a sequence of favorable conditions) kisses those who persevere and stay true to their dreams.

Thinking positively and constructively really causes positive conditions and events to take place so that our wishes take form and come true. Scientific studies conducted in Munich, at the Max Planck Institute of Neurobiology, confirm that the human brain is much more alert, and fixes objectives in the long term, when it is positively stimulated. And this happens through positive feelings. Conversely, we work (that is, our mind works) at its worst under negative impulses and feelings. Similarly, we can also affirm that we cause negative results when we think negative or no results at all!

Mind conditioning (employed in the military, Secret Service, and religious sects, all over the world and not always under very happy circumstances) is a reality and is based on imprinting our mind with certain goals. When we "program" ourselves to pursue a certain goal, then we achieve it as a result of attuned and focused actions.

Others may say that we are an integrant part of God, God's particles, and that **we do not only participate in the infinity of the Universe, but we are indeed the Universe,** this last being a sort of infinite organism where all things are interconnected and already existing. Then, by responding to the simple dogma "**ask, believe, receive,**" we can manifest anything we want, from big money to the ideal partner—just by thinking of it. **Thoughts are believed to make things material, in that they are the energy that moves the universe and is at the base of creation.**

Until now, I personally find nothing that I cannot accept and include in my own catalogue of beliefs. I am not religious, but I am deeply spiritual. In my opinion, a person who does not give room to spirituality is a person who can hardly reach an inner balance. And I deem spiritual also those people who simply ask themselves how and why they live in the here and now but can get no valid explanation for themselves.

In the end, the scientific world has also accepted that there can be multiple theories, multiple realities. **Multiplicity is indeed the new way of observing reality**, in contrast to the way in the past the scientific world has addressed it—that is, by exclusion.

The fact is that like any other thing on the earth, **we are made not only out of matter, but also out of energy**. Think of the structure of an atom; a nucleus with neutrons and electrons orbiting around it. ORBITING! A lot of free space filled with energy that keeps these microsystems together. Atoms make molecules, which make cells, which make our body; we are more ethereal than we think! This energy is real. An **energy field** is able to interact with other energy fields and create changes in them. It is just necessary for them to come close to one another. It is through the **vibrations or waves** these energy fields send that things communicate with things, or human bodies with things, or things with human bodies, so that it is believed that if you are tuned to the same wavelength of something, you receive that something in the same way your radio receives the morning news. If we are negatively loaded, we attract negativity. Conversely, if we are positively loaded, we attract positivity.

How many times have you felt a person coming close to you although you were turned away? It can be particularly true when we like someone very much and he or she is approaching us: it is as if the air between could be cut into slices! Isn't it? Or is it that we like them very much because our energy fields (or Auras, or Souls, or whatever name you want to give them) are compatible, in that they send each other the same kind of vibrations?

Again, many are the theories existing (a lot more than those I listed, indeed) and supporting, in different but not at all conflicting ways, the validity of positive thoughts and their mastering role in the realization of our projects. Moreover, it is reported that they are able to reverse the worst destinies ever and **heal incurable illnesses**. Personally, I would take this allegation with caution, especially when it comes to choosing between traditional medicine and alternative ways to treat cancer and other life-threatening diseases.

A study has been recently carried out on ex-terminal patients who had miraculously recovered from their deadly diseases. They came from very different backgrounds (different culture, religion, race, gender, education, etc.). They were directly asked what their life was like and what they did that could explain or be linked to their recovery. Three answers were common to all of them: 1. "I pray or ask repeatedly to stay alive"; 2. "I enjoy every moment of my life and smile a lot"; and 3. "I thank God or fate every day for keeping me alive" (one of them has been doing it for thirty years already!). Among them are small farmers living in isolation and people with a low degree of education who had never heard about the power of the mind, self-development, motivation coaching, or whatsoever. They were just determined not to die. They asked it. They believed it. They obtained it. Coincidences? Very interesting. Accompanying strong desire and faith were feelings of happiness (that *"laughter is the best medicine"* is widely known—otherwise sleepy muscles are activated, vessels walls are strengthened, blood flow is accelerated) and gratitude, which made their wishes detectable by their subconscious. Their subconscious then activated the healing process to complete recovery. This is what the scientists concluded. **Our *subconscious mind* undertakes for us a number of incredibly complex tasks** while we are engaged in our daily activities, and we just do not care about it. For example, breathing, remaining alert against accidents, and healing wounds (which is collecting, organizing, and managing millions of different cells deputed to the transportation, elimination, and substitution of necrotized tissues) organizes our knowledge and memories, etc. Subconscious and conscious minds are not able to communicate with each other—or better, not in a direct way that allows the conscious to control the subconscious. And this is good, since life-sustaining functions would be otherwise be challenged by our own will! What makes the subconscious sensitive about what we want is repetition (we are now back to conditioning!) and a strong positive feeling (as already said) as a combo. **Prayers—** think about it—are nothing but a repetition of what we want, reinforced by faith. This is the reason why sometimes so-called "miracles" follow intense prayers! A very strong feeling (you have to burn with desire, to shiver just thinking of it!) for something you want to achieve, be it a car or a good divorce, for example, is what you need to achieve them. Then determination, focus, and action will follow without any particular effort because you are simply inspired. It does not work if you strongly wish your ex-spouse to have an accident or get cancer so that he or she disappears. It seems it works only when you are good willed and when your goals are in harmony with those of other people. So do not even try to!

I can tell you what my personal experience in this respect is: whenever I had a dream and it literally burned inside me (with creative thoughts and ideas waking me up in the middle of the night), it became reality. I have really gotten everything I wanted under these circumstances—my own companies, the car, and other goals I set forth in my life. When I was too busy, too influenced or subdued or mentally unaware, to notice what I really wanted and lost track of my dreams, then the most unthinkable and undesirable situations have entered my life. Therefore, there is a strict **connection and interactivity between happiness, Self, and creation**—as it happens in the realm of nature, where new life comes from the union of two orgasming organisms, be they plants or animals.

Determination is something you cannot fake. It must come from inside. Motivation disappears and produces no mechanical movement toward action when your Self is not "personally" involved in the process of creation. Sooner or later you are tired of sticking with something you do not believe in. Again, it only comes from within, and it comes when *your* dreams and *your* goals are aligned, not when *your* goals are aligned with *someone else's* dreams.

By dreaming, you feel alive, strong, and happy. This is the most fertile ground to plant new seeds. Therefore, now you understand a little better why even in this particular situation, you just need to switch the dreams *on* to start producing positive changes! I am convinced it is in our nature, that this power belongs to us. **We bring inside a world of incredible skills.** In some ways, we have forgotten or misused or ignored them so far, and some have disappeared. Certain survival instincts, for example, that belong to animals, plants, and man as well, get lost in our species after six months of age (natural reflexes such as climbing, grabbing, or swimming). It is also believed that babies establish telepathic connections to their mothers in order to get what they need. And actually, I know for sure that my child never had to cry to obtain what it wanted up to kindergarten age. I have always, amazingly, understood and responded accordingly. The drama is that we lose our instinctive behaviors and skills as soon as the learning process starts. And the more we learn and let the external world take root in our brains, the less contact we have with our original nature.

That does not mean that this original nature and substance has disappeared! Not at all. It is there, as a whole set of opportunities. And if an autistic person succeeds in accurately reproducing the map of Manhattan after just taking a short look at it, or another can automatically calculate amazingly long and complicated equations in milliseconds, then the human brain really has unlimited capacities. There are also people who possess a high IQ, whose abilities (which are often trained and further improved) are incredible for, and go beyond the range of, everybody with a normal IQ. For example, remembering 1400 different numbers in the right sequence was the last feat performed by a German lawyer in a Mastermind world championship. Autistic individuals display special capacities and a lack of social competencies. They have no feelings and have to learn to show responses (which is reacting to love, affection etc., as everybody expects of them as people) in order to be socially integrated. Famous autistic persons were Mozart, Einstein, Jefferson, Newton, Michelangelo... Curious, isn't it? Then perhaps the allegation that learning processes, social conditioning, and education crush and destroy the control we have on the mind is true! If those (see above) who are impervious to feelings and social pressures remain virgin and can use their original powers, then papas, mamas, professors, colleagues, superiors, the president of United States, etc., in their attempt to make of us better individuals, in reality are clipping our wings.

Now it can be more apparent to you how important the Questionnaire (that you have completed as a tool to contact your Self and keep in touch with it) is. **Inside you resides the power to do everything you want!**

If you belong to a Christian church, you will find confirmation of that in the words of Jesus. He stated with the Trinity "Father, Son, and Holy Spirit" the concept of coexistence and blending of flesh and divine. Ancient Greek gods behaved as humans, although they possessed supernatural powers. So, no one can be scandalized or feel blasphemous by stating that every person, embodying a part of God, is a God him- or herself. According to this dogma, we should be able to produce any reality we want. That is, we have the ability to manifest our thoughts—to turn them into matter.

I do not know if you can believe it or not. Nor am I asking you to do it. It is not that important because apart from the multiplicity of religious, philosophic, and scientific explanations, there are you and your life, your will, your own abilities. And these can be recognized and used independently from any external belief. They belong to you like your hands or your eyes.

Personally, I take assumptions as true as soon as they become statistically strong and evident. At times I am a sort of St. Thomas and even need to see and touch myself to believe. There are simply too many people who assert they use their will and thoughts to get what they want, and I am among them. I have always made use of a strong will, even as a child. Instinctively. My mother often reported my having a conversation with a little friend of mine when I was five. I told him with extreme authority and self-confidence these precise words: "If you want something, you must insist and insist and insist until you get it! I do so, and I always obtain what I want!" I get goose bumps. What determination for a child aged five!

I always had dreams, and when I was focused, I obtained what I wanted. And this is just the right way to produce realities. Ending up solving that particular problem, having that job, or conquering that particular partner is always a matter of thinking and pursuing. I was interested to know how it worked, though. I read tons of books and articles, attended live and web seminars, and learned from different sources, old and new, movements of thought that had been created—all the possible theories and explanations relevant to this phenomenon. All that has not changed the fact itself that our thoughts are at the base of creation. Though the more are you aware of it, the better are you in control of it. Control implies the mastering of a phenomenon, and this is what I am trying to convey throughout this book.

Nature is perfect. It has created perfect systems. Evolution has technically and precisely responded to many different life forms so that they can cope with changes in their environment. Think also about flowers' and animals' attributes, about their incredible interactions so that they can help one another complete their life cycles and assure the continuity of their species. We are just part of this perfection!

Now, after having realized the scopes of your existence, and having built a tool to visualize them (the vision board or written document containing your dreams), **you are no longer watching what happens in your life. You are starting to create it!**

Tuning Your Thoughts and Trusting Your Perceptions to Obtain the Life You Want

Always stay attuned and true to your Self and your desires without betraying them. Letting go as soon as obstacles are impeding your path can turn out to be a very bad mistake; the arrival is often a few meters away, around the corner. **Once you have set forth your goals, it is advisable to stick to them until you have attained them.** It brings no good to change plans every two weeks. In fact, a fantastic mechanism in your brain is switched on when you want something strongly and intend to fulfill your desire, provided you give it time to work. Let me explain. Your subconscious is like a good mother, and it makes sure that your body functions properly. Also, it takes care that your emotional life is fulfilled—in a word, that you are content. It has, however, no way to establish whether this contentment is right or not (think about addictions, for example). The subconscious doesn't think—it operates! It is your conscious mind that tells you, based on your education, experiences, and so on, what is good or not good to do. Back to the subconscious mind, when your feelings about something you wish are so strong that you can reach its wavelength (it is not as easy as ordering a pizza over the phone!), it starts engaging actions targeted to your wishes and thoughts by alerting and putting your sins and skills to work. **Example: You dream of a job in Paris.** Paris and aspects of its life and architecture, such as the Eiffel Tower or the nice bistros at Saint Germaine become constant thoughts, pivotal issues in your mind. You find yourself instinctively Googling "Paris" to get more and more information about it. You suddenly start to notice a number of things around you that are linked with Paris (people speaking French, French fries, French autos, French clothing, French perfumes, etc.). Even while thinking of other things and keeping busy with your usual activities, your subconscious continues to run, in the background, the program aimed at fulfilling your wish to go to and work in Paris. You have not even started to look for a job in Paris, but voila, while riding the subway, your eyes go through two meters of corridor and end up on a half-page newspaper ad: they are seeking for someone with your job skills, **in Paris**. After a successful interview, you barely have the time to organize your moving;

you are catapulted into your new life in Paris. Without your noticing it, your subconscious has transformed you into a receiver, putting all your sins at service of your inner goal. This is only an example of how it works. No fairy tale. When we are interested in something, our beautiful mind starts to be alert.

It can also happen for smaller things that seem to have no importance but awaken our interest.

Another example: My father lives about 1500 miles away from me. He recently bought a new auto, an SUV (Sport Utility Vehicle). I did not even know there was a class of autos named this way, but from the time my father got his, my eyes started to notice more and more of them—a lot of them! I realized that a good 10 percent of autos in my neighborhood are indeed SUVs. And in parking lots, I often happen to park beside a SUV. I had lived my entire life without SUVs, and then they all came to the surface, all of a sudden! Again, this is only one of the ways our subconscious mind works for us. And we can take advantage of this quality by indulging in the thoughts that are important to us. Do thoughts mold our reality? No doubt—they do!

Use your new awareness and enjoy your time from now on. Never before has there been so much potential in your future. You are now going to mold your life the way you would like it to be, and this process of creation is simply fantastic and exciting!

Be alert, receptive, and ready to catch and use the suggestions, hints, and positive conditions that your mind will be putting at your service from time to time. Do not be afraid to start new ventures, new projects. Change is part of our nature and a quality of each particle of our body. It would be a pity to let your fears stop the positive life-energy flow deputed to keep you "alive and kicking." **One of the most powerful opponents of happiness is indeed fear.** Unfortunately, the chains that bind people to their comfortable mediocrity are the same ones that bind their future to an unsuccessful destiny. **The courage to dream is the very first step. LISTENING TO YOUR DREAMS is the second!**

I do really believe in a world where everything is possible. As a perfect mix of spirituality and scientific earthiness, I feel free to retain everything I deem positive and constructive for my life, regardless of its provenience. On the other hand, some people might refuse to embrace new life concepts just because of their general disbelief or because their religious faith narrows their sights. They tend to respond *"It's not for me"* and prevent new concepts from positively influencing their lives. Therefore, I hope you are not hindered in your self-development work by any form of skepticism.

First, it is important that you really believe in and trust yourself. You possess the power to leave behind unpleasant situations by focusing on your own dreams and on the life that you want, which starts right now.

Wake up every morning with a beautiful, refreshing sense of expectation! What you experience as painful now can in reality hide a change for the better. Let me tell you an anecdote (I have experienced hundreds of these). After unsuccessfully searching for a new home for seven months, I was finally at the point of signing a rental contract for a beautifully located, nice apartment at the edge of a park. Apart from being smaller than I required, it looked perfect. Then, one second before he signed the contract, while he was holding the pen, the owner changed his mind and decided to keep the apartment free for his weekends in town. Surprisingly (most of worst and best things come by surprise), instead of feeling depressed, while driving back home I felt a sense of tranquility come to my heart, and it told me: *"You will find a better one soon, a bigger home you do not have to compromise for. This is the only reason why you didn't get that one!"* And in fact, only one week later, I found the home of my dreams, near the center, with twice the number of rooms as the previous one and a big garden and cellar. The ideal home for me, my ex, my dogs, and our future children! Furthermore, the price was (again) surprisingly under the market average. I got it, of course, notwithstanding that one hundred other couples had visited that same apartment.

Never lose your mind in difficult situations. You might have heard this saying a thousand times, but indeed it is true that there is always a light at the end of the tunnel! This is confirmed daily by millions of people who set their minds free for positive thoughts and get results. The world belongs to those who think and act positive! You may need to cry at times or to scream. Then do it—it can be relieving. But never cry or be angry too long! You may want to dedicate your time and energies in more pleasing and rewarding ways.

ALL WHAT YOU HAVE TO KNOW AND DO TO KILL DIVORCE STRESS

I am whole, perfect, strong, powerful, loving, harmonious and happy.

- Charles F. Haanel 1866 - 1949

Writer, businessman, member of the American Society of Physical Research

Divorce can affect your mental balance up to the point that a wide variety of nervous disorders may occur, ranging from panic attacks, depression, burnout, and psychosomatic illnesses, up to overreacting to any further problems that come your way so that you lose control of your life or part of it. All the procedures linked to a divorce are incredibly energy consuming. And this is a matter of fact. **Hence, our strategy is to save and even multiply your energies.** You are abandoning a painful highway and are going to feel lighter, happier, and conscious of your own strengths.

First: Calm Down!

This can be achieved in different ways, and the good news is that these are all pleasant. Then, if you exchange a considerable amount of correspondence and have numerous meetings and calls with legal advisors, public authorities, and so on and so forth, assign this information and these calls and meetings a limited time and space in your mind and in your schedule. I have opened my own correspondence with my lawyer only when I was calm enough to read it, but also soon enough not to get haunted by it. Do not postpone. Work at solving your problems as soon as they come; otherwise they pile up and look even drearier, more or less like a *black, sticky mass of tar*. This does not mean you will be always able to manage them in holy tranquility. Divorce can be a hard, nerve-tensing process, particularly when you're married to a shark.

Sustainable Self-Development - Happiness and Control

Overreacting is also normal. You are not a guru, nor are you expected to become one. Most personal coaches advise you to control your reactions and maintain your poise in extreme situations. This would be nice! Some mentors warn that if you do not control your wildness, your wildness will control you. This is right! I agree. But I also think that self-development must be an attainable goal, which everyone can get—hot Latinos and cold Nordic people alike, so to speak. **It is not by containing your rage, but by increasing your inner peace, that you are gradually able to control bad or wild emotions. Self-development must be sustainable,** otherwise it remains just theory, something for selling books and making people plunge into the perennial dichotomy of humanity and perfection. If you start reading Buddha's affirmations expecting in a weekend to become impervious to all the negative feelings listed in the English Oxford Dictionary, you might get disillusioned and think that you will never be able to reach higher level of **consciousness. But this is the problem—most of our reactions start in our unconscious mind, and you are able to talk to it and influence it positively using mainly the language of feelings, as we saw.** Blocking rage is good, and you are also able to do it in a number of ways and a number of times (not always, though). But preventing it from being generated is the key to successful, 100 percent control! This is achievable through a happy, light-hearted subconscious mind. Inner happiness or balance is the very cornerstone of self-development. Happiness supports enthusiasm and empowers creativity and initiative. Happiness makes you a better person in your private, family, and work spheres. Happiness keeps you healthy and lets you stick to your plans. You have to cultivate happiness as if it were the most precious flower in your garden.

Control over your mind through happiness will also ensure that the quest for inner healing does not affect your empathy; some people push themselves too far and start living in parallel realities. Happiness has the quality of wanting to be shared, so that everyone in your family will take advantage of it, along with colleagues, neighbors, friends, and all the people who come in contact with you. You will be more prone to love, to socialize, to take risks. You will be vibrating happiness, shedding light all over. The power of your words will be enhanced, thanks to your new charisma. In this status of enlightenment, you will be hardly put down by life. And should it happen, you will be able to stand up again and fight hard the next round.

Facing Disappointment

Back to sustainable self-development, which respects your human nature and can be embraced by everyone, if you need to vent, to scream out a couple of bad words at time, do it! Do you need to cry? Cry! If you need to release negative energies, then explode (provided that nobody is nearby). But then stop and turn your mind to the next pleasant thing to do. Do not deliver yourself to utter pain. Let no black curtain go down on you. Let nobody and nothing KO you—not those you have loved and who now make you suffer.

Do not let your problems abuse you. They are problems, and every problem has a solution, or more than one. If you feel scared and panicky, immediately use your swirling smoke ball visualization exercise and then get busy with something you like to do until you feel better. In the second part of this book, I give you a more-than-extensive guide on how to improve your mental wellness so that you will no longer feel helpless when you are disappointed.

Many people are long-distance commuters; they jump from appointment to appointment, master efficiency at work, are available for their children, and have a brilliant social life. During divorce, you need extra mental and physical efforts to keep up with schedules (yours and those of your work-children-connections and eventually house-garden-pets) and still be fit for the duels with your ex (if ex is not a jerk, I am glad of it!). For many of these beautiful people, divorce is a nightmare, and the borderline between "I hold on" and "I can't anymore" is a daily issue. The goals you set forth in the previous chapter and outlined in your vision board or document are a fundamental instrument to keep your attention focused on the very core of your life. If you take the time to look at them every morning, you will remind yourself of your priorities and refresh your soul. These will shine like gold against your divorce, particularly as soon as you start to realize that you are doing great. You will naturally slow down and minimize your stress as soon the picture of your divorce blurs under the light of your successes. I am sure nothing is more rewarding and can make you more self-confident than the results you get. They have a big resonance on your subconscious: you feel happy and thankful, a perfect combo emitting such positive vibrations that you will attract even more of that. When you start to become a recipient of positivity, your efforts to keep the virtual circle running will be minimal.

Your Brand-New HD World

Once you know for sure that your life has taken a positive turn and you are empowered to literally "create" your life, you will also start to see the world in HD. Your sensitivity, perceptions, and awareness of what happens around you, of the mechanisms that regulate people's thinking, of the way they react, and even of the common little things that never attracted your interest before (such the wonderful blond hot dog seller around the corner, the white lilies in your neighbor's little pond, or the yellow tie of the milkman, which originally belonged to Michael Jackson). You enjoy the light caressing your desk at work. Your department head's face looks not so grim after all—you even saw a smile today. Your neighbor has offered to look after your children while you go to the theater with your best friend or new encounter. You know, the more you spread love—to things, vegetables, animals, people, and whatever—the more you receive. Love generates magic results—a terrific new good feeling to be added to your virtual circle!

Boomerang Effect: Giving Love

I am used to giving love to my plants and to my pets, and it seems I have a certain luck with them. They are loved, and they live and reproduce in my home as if in their natural settings. I caress them and thank them for gifting me with their beauty, for bringing harmony and comfort to me and my home. I thank my pets for always being by my side (not my fishes, which remain in their aquarium) and for bringing me peace, love, and happiness. I am trustful, open, and social. I can always take a step back if the person I have to deal with is unfair or hurts me. This positive, loving attitude toward living beings grants enormous tranquility. I feel aligned with my principles of openness and respect too, and I am so at peace with myself that I really never have problems going to sleep in the evening. I have nothing to blame myself for, and consequently I go to bed with no worries in my mind. Sleeping well is essential, as we will see in the next sections, particularly when you have to deal with the stress of coping with divorce.

In Essence:

Love has one thousand forms and recipients' faces:

ঌ When you give love, you are also more receptive to love.

ঌ Your perceptions are positively amplified.

ঌ You notice things, details, phenomena, people, qualities, living beings, etc. that never caught your attention before.

ঌ These subjects enrich you with their presence and existence and so doing, they give love back to you—the boomerang effect.

By loving, we release serotonin, commonly named *happiness hormones*. And while we romantically speculate about love and its positive effects on our social life, our body transforms a biological process into a wonderful spiritual Eden.

Among all of your love recipients, there, in the first line, you must put yourself. Take the time to dedicate yourself to the things you like to do or to take care of. They are presumably also included in your Vision board if they are not part of your actual experience yet. **Pamper** yourself up to the point of becoming a little egoistic. Put an end to your endless availability and introduce into your timetable an oasis of tranquility and pleasure "for you only."

Repeat as often as you can the following affirmation by Charles F. Haanel: *"I am whole, perfect, strong, powerful, loving, harmonious and happy."* It does not mean that you are not going to make mistakes again in the future. Falling down is part of our human nature. But we are also made so perfect that we can stand up again and again and again, each time even stronger than before. This is your perfection, and no one and nothing can take it away!

Twenty-Eight Golden Suggestions to Manage the Stress of Divorce

1. Happy Divorce

Keep yourself at a safe distance or away from negative sources.

Avoid films, TV daily news, and newspapers reporting crimes, mankind problems, wars, cruel images of violence, and so on. You have enough problems right now.

2. Happy Divorce

Take a holiday from sticky, negative, depressed friends, family members, and colleagues—that is, people who are only able to criticize the whole world, and nothing works, and their partners are the worst, and they are just unable to make any decisions without consulting you. You think you are the center of their universe, but indeed they are simply exploiting you. They call you in the middle of the night because the heating does not work, and they do not come to the logical conclusion that one or two more blankets are enough to sleep warmly till daylight, when it will be possible to call the caretaker. They do not pay any attention to your need for support or your need to stay tranquil in this time of your life. They just go on pretending and putting themselves at the center of "your world." Tell them you are in a hurry and you cannot listen to them. They have been sucking your energies all the time, and now that your energies are low and you need to be supported and pampered, you still have to play the role of the stronger one. These are reverse-charge relationships, where you always pay the bill. They consume your positive energies and give you absolutely nothing back. They infect you with their bad mood and leave you totally drained. Learn to recognize this sort of "energy sucking people" and avoid contacts with them. You are no Mother Teresa nor a social hero; not at this time. They are also never minimally thankful of your efforts in their direction. They are terribly selfish and will eventually react very badly to your lack of attention, but this is what you want to achieve—**distance**! Please do not feel guilty.

They will find soon a substitute and will throw their trash into someone else's life, since they are dependent.

3. Happy Divorce

Extra hours? No, thank you! Do not take more work than you actually can carry out. Time and energy are to be effectively shared between your public and private sphere. If you are afraid you could lose your job by no longer granting extra hours to your boss, then you may want to re-evaluate thoroughly what you wish to have as a job. It may be one that does not challenge your private life. The problem should not be there as soon as you meet a new partner. There are nonrisky ways to look around for a new job while you maintain your present one. If you are content with it, no problem. You will be able to adjust things at work so that you are not overwhelmed by it. You will use your will and thoughts positively in that direction.

4. Happy Divorce

Shut out continual noises—drilling machines, traffic, etc. If you are not able to shut them out by closing your windows, or they are an integral part of your work environment, you might want to wear earplugs for a while to help to calm your nerves.

5. Happy Divorce

Memories are like quicksand. Under memories I also include that special song that reminds you of the times you were happy with your ex; objects, clothes, perfumes, music— anything can transport you to your past life with him or her, when everything was so lovely and perfect. Now it is time to make a place for your new loved one, existing or future, and he or she will not be eager to be confronted with reminders of your past relationship. Furthermore, the longer you stick to your ex, the harder is your way to love happiness. You are warmly advised to remove everything that reminds you of your ex-spouse—you will be doing yourself a big favor.

6. Happy Divorce

Give up or dramatically reduce tobacco, alcohol, and drugs. They are no good, and they weaken your brain to the point that you do not even control 10 percent of your life. Now you have the chance to show your value, to yourself and to all the people around who are waiting for you to sink. Adverse and complicated situations light up volcanic reactions inside human beings (Paradox Effect), as it happens when you have the flu and your immune system starts fighting against bacteria and viruses. The mechanism is similar, only it takes place inside your subconscious mind. You have pure energy to be used against the negativities and in favor of new healthy habits. There are a lot of ways to give up bad habits, but none will work if you do not entirely embrace them. Again, no time is more suitable than this to get rid of an addiction. You can try it alone or find help in the appropriate fora (self-help communities online and offline, health centers, etc.).

7. Happy Divorce

Avoid everything that gives you a sense of uneasiness. You are often right in judging a situation with your heart. Pondering too much can really be a con. If I think of all the times I made bad decisions, they were right when it resulted from long rumination. When I became engaged to my ex-husband, I sensed it was not such a good idea and I took time to decide (1 month!), but more rational considerations led me astray.

8. Happy Divorce

Say no and mean it! People, from your boss to your children, sometimes insist on trying to obtain something from you at all costs (your costs!). They put you under pressure directly or through the finest blackmail so that you say yes in the end. Now it is over. A no is a no, and no room must be left for further "negotiations." Your children will benefit from an assertive, happier, and peppy parent, which is better than a compliant and burned-out one. Say NO to whoever tries to change your mind above your threshold of tolerability.

9. Happy Divorce

Go out and have fun. If you like dancing or going to arts events or fishing or whatever, do it! If you have children, get your ex to look after them when you are away, or call a babysitter.

10. Happy Divorce

Nothing is more inspiring and calming than nature. The sight of nature is as touching as the sight of a baby—it positively penetrates your heart. Everything that has to do with it, from taking a walk in a park to adopting new plants for your apartment/balcony/garden, helps you feel more integrated with the universe. You can also bring green to your workplace or enjoy being close to water (which has also an enormous calming effect). Again, if you are not able to regularly visit water places, such as a sea or a lake or a river, equip your home and/or your workplace with an aquarium or an indoor Zen fountain. Should you have no idea how to take care of an aquarium and you do not want to learn it, a Zen fountain is a better choice—you do not want tropical fishes to suffer or die for your tranquility's sake.

11. Happy Divorce

PERFORMING and FIGURATIVE ARTS: Play music or play an instrument. If you are not able to, you might want to learn. While playing an instrument, no matter how good you are, you convey your feelings with your instrument. This is very liberating, since in a few minutes you can release a lot of negative tension. Musicians cannot live without their instruments, and they always travel (also privately) together with their own instruments; the therapeutic effect of their music makes them sort of addicted. Music finds its way to reach you not only through your ears, but also through your bones and your cells, which are put in motion by its waves, with amazing effects on the psyche. Therefore, it is preferable to play or listen to fewer or no melancholic pieces while divorcing, and opt for calming, energizing, inspiring music that meets your tastes. Natural clangs are very good too, especially to meditate. **Dancing or painting is liberating too, as well as writing poems or whatever.** All activities involving creativity, which channel your emotions outward, are great to ease your frustrations (if any!) and decrease the stress of divorce. Art is freedom, and you can make whatever you want with an instrument, with your feet, with your pen, or with your canvas. Think how happy and calm children are while they are absorbed in their drawings, for example. You can paint your sun blue, or draw plant species that do not exist. Do not forget, though, to keep your sense of reality; if your bills pile up and you do not earn your money as a performer/dancer/poet/painter etc., then it might be that more dedication to job goals is needed.

12. Happy Divorce

Keep a regular sleep schedule. Depending on your age, you need from five to eight hours a day of sleep. There is also scientific evidence that a twenty-minute nap can refresh your body and your mind. Too long a nap during the day might on the contrary affect your daily performance negatively. Ideally, you should regularly and sufficiently sleep at night, in a silent and dark room, and need no naps at all. Lack of sleep dramatically decreases all of your perceptions and abilities. This results in an effort to compensate and creates further stress. You really do not need at this time to lose sleep and the capacity to properly react to adversities (if any). Discipline is required so that you can still enjoy life—and nightlife—without paying too high a price.

13. Happy Divorce

Take your time and learn to plan your activities. Keep a regular agenda for your family and private appointments, allowing enough time before and after each event. You do not need to run like a marathon man in between.

14. Happy Divorce

If you have children, regularly do something that pleases you ALL. Perfect parents tend to reduce their interests and hobbies to a minimum in order to be able to meet their children's needs and wants. That happened to me too. Then I realized I could do both! Cinema, for example: I used to take my child only to children's movies. Now, at times, my daughter enjoys "normal" movies that are appropriate to her age (of course!). The same happened with theater and classical concerts. I look for afternoon events where I can bring my daughter with me. She gets inspiration and may discover new likes and dislikes, and I can enjoy my hobbies and my child's company at the same time. Do something at least **twice a week that is *suitable* for your children and that YOU like very much**.

15. Happy Divorce

Reduce your household chores. There are electric appliances in almost every house—i.e., a washing machine, a dryer, a dishwasher, and a microwave. These alone help every household keep up with the very fast pace of modern times. But now there are even more intelligent electric appliances that further reduce the time we have to spend doing heavy chores. And I have found a really great difference between the time I used to rely only on the basics, and the time since I equipped myself with additional domestic appliances. An intelligent dryer also saves me time for ironing because it takes care of every kind of textile and clothing, such as blankets, cushions, and so on; an automatic intelligent coffee machine allows me to just press a button to obtain a broad range of coffee drinks (from cappuccino to espresso to latte macchiato, etc.); and last but not least, my new great love! It is something I really heartily advise you to buy even if you have to make installments: a hovering robot. There are so many brands on the market, it is sometimes difficult to choose. My dear hovering robot (it really attracts tender feelings, so good and effective it is!) is truly intelligent: it hovers efficiently, not randomly, in that it scans the floor, reaches every corner, goes under the sofas, cleans the carpets, warns of blockages (it can speak!), and as soon as the battery goes low, it connects to its loading unit to restart working from the point where it had to break. Just fantastic! This is exactly what you expect from a robot: a total ability to perform tasks independently.

I like cooking, and consequently I rely on a complete series of cooking aids in my kitchen. This is not mandatory, but **if you equip your household with washing machine, dryer, microwave, dishwasher, and hovering robot, then you can spend your time more**

creatively and effectively than cleaning. And as a result, you will be and also look more relaxed. Household chores have never made anyone look younger!

16. Happy Divorce

Nutritional supplements such as magnesium and B Vitamins can help your nervous system to better recover from or cope with a significant amount of stress. Also under the best circumstances and conditions, a divorce always implies an increased number of concerns, burdens, and duties. If you are not alcohol and/or drug addicted and you have regular and adequate meals (that is, containing all the basic nutrients and not excessive in fats and sugar), you and your brain should be already in a condition to work properly, without resorting to supplements. You can take a chamomile tea in the evening before going to sleep if your day was particularly stressful. **I am strongly against dietary supplements that are not strictly required, particularly when consumed in huge quantities.** The body has to do extra work to assimilate them, and when they are too much, intoxication can be a consequence. Also, nervousness badly affects the digestive system, which often reacts with reflux, stomach cramps, or evacuation problems. A simple and effective solution is probiotic and intestinal flora capsules. They are easy to take (if you do not like yogurt particularly, for example) and have no side effects. I regularly take three capsules a day of a very complete complex, which is not really cheap but is really effective. You may have to wait up to two weeks before you see improvements, and this is because bacteria gently repair your intestinal walls, fight the bad flora that has settled inside your intestines, and normalize consistency while easing evacuation. The importance of keeping your digestive system healthy and functioning is tremendous. Most part of your immune system is located inside it. You can prevent a lot of major disorders and illnesses from worsening your delicate stress level just by maintaining good digestion.

17. Happy Divorce

Rejuvenating and stress fighting hormones (testosterone, etc.) are never a solution; often, they are prescribed without ascertaining whether you really need them (there are no standards, really, pro capita or pro sex or pro age, since everyone has his or her own level to work properly). Hormone therapies saw their best times in the nineties. Afterward, due to a series of fatal cases deriving from misuse and overdoses, pharmaceutical companies and physicians who made terrific money out of that concept started to put a brake to prescriptions. For decades, researchers have been busy with the question: "Why do men live on average five years less than women?" The answer comes these days as one of the most sensational news items in the medical field. It has been found that testosterone is the factor responsible for a lower life expectancy in men. Consequently, hormones are really the worst remedy you can think of when you want to introduce more power, youth, or balance in your life. A couple of coffees a day are enough to keep alert, and vitamins are to be found in all fruits and vegetables.

18. Happy Divorce

Visualization and hypnosis are a valid way to calm down and make your natural resources (which are infinite, believe me!) available. There are many products on the market that are enjoyable and that will save you money on medical bills. Mobile and tablet applications, for example, are portable and easy to use provided you do not practice visualization or hypnosis while driving or operating machines. If you use them before going to bed, they can greatly improve the quality of your sleep and the work of your subconscious during the night. You can buy as many products (CDs, apps, books) as you want, but remember that it is not advisable to overwhelm the mind with new instructions every day. Hypnosis and visualization need time to be effective. It is better to choose one or two products to use regularly. If you play a different exercise each time, your mind could overreact to "instruction" overload and not perform as expected.

19. Happy Divorce

There are also very interesting ways to relax by controlling your **brain waves**. The brain emits different waves during its performance, and they are measurable (by electroencephalography) and classified into theta, beta, alpha, delta, and gamma. Each has a particular frequency and reproduces at a certain number of cycles; for example, delta waves occur while sleeping and reproduce at 1/2 - 4 cycles per second). These can be regulated almost on demand by listening to **"binaural beats,"** which are available on the market as MP3s. There are also PC programs and apps that allow you to change settings and other features and be more in control of what you are hearing. This is not science fiction, just another opportunity that I also used, although at present it is considered more entertaining than scientific. Anyway, I found some MP3s and an app that was very helpful. There are programs to "activate" your brain and others that are meant to put it on a meditation wavelength. Their ability to reach your subconscious and make you experience astral trips is an object of speculation. I never tested nor experienced this last possibility. Anyway, by searching "binaural waves" and/or "brainwaves" or "brain waves" on YouTube, you will find a great number of gratis sources. You need headphones and no worries about side effects.

20. Happy Divorce

Meditation is the mother of all relaxing/calming methods and practices, although it is not limited to relaxation only. What is very good about it is that a lot of different meditation techniques exist, suitable for all tastes and needs. Flash meditation, for example, is for people living on the treadmill: it puts your mind at rest and loads it with energy and focus in only one second. These results are not to be expected the first time you try it. This is a discipline, and as such, you need time to master it. You can practice meditation everywhere (while commuting, before an important meeting, or while sitting on the toilet, for example). At the base of meditation, there is the ability to "abandon" the physical world so that the problems connected with it are left behind. You open yourself to a host of new perceptions that come from within or from nature and the universe. The effects of meditation are tremendous in fighting stress and nervous disorders, and in feeling reinvigorated. For a Happy, Divorced Person, meditation is a strongly recommended instrument to maintain good mental health while coping with the mostly unpleasant situations linked to a divorce. You feel fresh and regenerated afterward, as if you had slept a whole night on angel feathers. Everyone can find his or her own meditation style. Read books, buy CDs, and search the Internet. Again, there are new digital supports that can help the less spiritual come closer to this discipline. There are, for example, PC programs using finger sensors that let you move inside virtual worlds and interact with them by using your mental focus. You are in command of those worlds and in command of your thoughts and emotions. I "played" a couple of times with one of these products until I managed to control every experience inside it, which made me more aware of my concentration abilities. Afterward, I found it no longer interesting or helpful for my further self-development or as a tool for meditation, since meditation goes really beyond a mind game.

Apart from these modern adult digital toys, old, traditional ways are always available and accessible to everybody (also to those who are not computer geeks) to unbind the force of nature inside them.

It is also important that you find yourself at ease while meditating because anything disturbing can compromise the results of a beginner. At a later stage, when you become a master in meditation, then you can do it wherever you are. There are some particularly inspiring places or settings for meditation. Those are places you find a special connection to (because they are particularly nice, for example, or because you find your peace there, or because they recall your childhood and you can unleash more creativity there, etc.). They can be indoor (a room, a sofa, a corner at work), or outdoors, within nature, and also in town. As a student, I had my meditation spot at the Tiberina Isle, in Rome. Not only was the place beautiful per se (magnificent ancient Roman architecture all around), but it was dense with immense spiritual energy. I felt really isolated from the city crowd and able to focus on the "nothing." I just felt inspired and recharged each time I needed some meditation, and although all around the traffic noise was really loud, I did not notice it.

Before testing flash or instant meditations, or any of the hundreds types and styles and possibilities available (yoga or chakra meditation, for example), I would advise you to start with a basic, natural, and traditional one.

Find a nice place to sit (in the lotus position if it does not bother you) and try this, just to begin:

Simple Meditation Exercise

Sit down and relax, keeping a natural, curved position, with your hands on your lap.

You do not have to feel the heaviness of your body.

Now take long and deep breaths. Do not force them to be too long. You will notice them becoming deeper and deeper.

Concentrate on every breath.

By regularly and naturally breathing, you will feel more and more relaxed. Continue to focus on your breathing for as long as you wish.

Then slowly stand up, stretch your arms and legs, and return to your regular occupation.

Repeat this at least once a day; each time you will experience something new. You can set a timer if you can dedicate only a limited time; in this case, it is advisable not to disturb your meditation by looking at your watch over and over again. As simple as it is, it can work wonders in your general mental wellness and in the way you respond to difficulties of any kind. Your mind needs restoration to work well. This I will repeat ad nauseum.

21. Happy Divorce

Flexibility. Wow, no word has been more abused than this in the last decades, in all fields. And in fact, it incorporates the most important of all survival functions. Only living species (animal and vegetal) with a high degree of flexibility, which is the capacity to quickly react and adapt to environmental changes, survive. This is a fact. Children's beloved dinosaurs were extinguished because of their inability to endure the big heat. Other smaller animals survived by evolving new features. Flexibility works selectively, in that a certain size might not be big enough to survive, or a certain speed can be too slow to survive. And since every day hundreds of animals and plants disappear from the earth's surface and will never come back, we do not want this to happen to you too—do we? And since we are learning how simple things or principles are vital to your position or situation, the best way to cope with divorce is to think flexibly and be ready to make any adjustments required to stay afloat—exactly like a buoy.

22. Happy Divorce

Don't Panic! The majority of our fears never become real. We are so threatened by them, though, that we become hypnotized. You are there, overwhelmed by "actual" plus "mighty" problems, and you go into a panic! Panicking is dangerous, since besides leaving you helpless and powerless, it brings you to what I call emergency decisions, which can badly affect your future and be reversible only at incredibly high costs. A very effective way to avoid going into a panic is to give yourself a little more time. If you do not find yourself at ease with a decision, wait for a while—one day or one week, depending on the importance of the decision. This does not mean you postpone it indefinitely, though. Time creates, and you might just need to leave it to work at your future according to your goals.

And **if you are panicking because you feel lonely and you think you never find someone to love again, you are right!** When you are panicking, no one will approach you except perhaps someone who just wants to take advantage of your temporary weaknesses; the world is full of vampires, eager to drink your blood, up to the last drop. I mean until you have nothing left, no self-esteem, no self-confidence, no love for anyone anymore. You are not desperate! **For this issue, you will find a lot of encouraging tips in Part 2 of this book**.

You do not need to panic! If you follow the advice I have given you and will give you later on, almost everything will start to move in your favor and in the right direction. And should something be still worrying you, this will be only a problem to solve, not a suicidal drama. You will get your poise and calm back. You can manage each and every difficulty, no matter how big. **You are adaptive and flexible. For every problem there is more than one acceptable solution. Stick to your dreams. Visualize them and keep them in your heart, night and day, and you will succeed in everything you want.**

23. Happy Divorce

The power of colors. There are some **details that make our day a little bit sunnier**, and at times they are apparently so small and irrelevant that rarely do we notice them or take them into account as making our world a better place. One of these small but powerful details are the colors we wear or which surround us (think about home textiles, for example). **In fact, our preferences of colors change during the years and are also subject to daily moods.** If your wardrobe is full of black clothes (or yellow, or plaid, or whatever; this is just an example) because twenty years ago you liked black very much, it might be no longer true, and you are just going on wearing this color by habit. Perhaps you are a more colorful person now, or you might still like dark colors, but earthly warm gold-browns instead of grey-to-black. Accessories can be very nice color highlights, conveying much better than anything else your feelings of the moment. Now I want you to use colors for the sake of your inner harmony. **What is the color that makes you happy and open hearted when you see it?** You can "feel" a color. It comes out when you, for example, handle an object with your favorite color. Then bring more joy in your life by wearing this color more often. Buy new clothes, accessories, and objects you use daily (such as cups, mugs, dishes, cushions, blankets, etc.) in that color. I like light blue/turquoise very much, and I feel immediately sunnier and lighthearted every time I wear this color. I had my living room painted in light blue, and I find joy and relaxation in my home like never before. Color and sunlight influence your mood and well-being, and the existence and practice of color therapy confirms this. It is known that people living in the north and enjoying the sunlight only a few hours a day in winter are more depressive and prone to suicide than Southerners. Sunlight lamps (reproducing the same wavelength and spectrum of sunlight) have invaded the consumer market and are no longer expensive luxury items. They can relieve this problem, but it would be even better to take advantage of natural daylight. In the chapter about home, you will find some more tips on this topic.

24. Happy Divorce

Shopping, massages, spas, sports clubs. YYYYESSSS, they make you really well. And it is no news that you have to pamper yourself to be happy and keep your mood high. You have already learned (here or before) to *think positive*, and this is simply great, but you also need *to make positive* things for yourself and breathe some luxury. If you do not have the financial means, especially now that you are submerged with bills, you can search the Internet for local promotions. There are always a number of possibilities to obtain free beauty and wellness treatments. Perhaps you have to drive or walk a bit longer than planned, but if a new fitness center has just opened and offers one trial day all inclusive (SPA included), and if you are low on money, you cannot miss this opportunity. You can become a real fox in this field, since by looking in local magazines, websites, and newspapers, you will find a lot of offers. Beauty treatments, sports facilities, and training, as well as a number of other "luxury" things, are offered for free during promotional campaigns.

Glamour has the sparkling effect of champagne. You can become more glamorous just by wearing golden twin cuffs or varnish shoes. Small accents can make you look younger—and also very important, FEEL YOUNGER. It is not bubbling, but rather embracing new and fantastic possibilities that thousands of people already know and use to make themselves special, interesting, and happy. Life is short, and we need to live the good, glamorous sides of it. After you have completed your duties at work and with the children (if any), then you can take time for yourself and become the King or the Queen you have always dreamed of!

25. Happy Divorce

Sports. I do not think I have to push sports high on your priorities list. Every good thing, though, must not be abused. In my old gym, a giant poster is hanging which showcases a smiling, attractive, slight-muscled young man with this caption: **"Less is more."** It seems that people have a tendency to become addicted to sports, or gyms, and can no longer think of other activities or hobbies. Their bodies are not better than those of others who are training once or twice a week. Their skin looks more grayish and yellowish than pink, and I can tell that they have on average more wrinkles than people who are not sporty at all. I really do not want to spend too many words here. But the fact is that when you put your body under too much (prolonged or repeated) physical strain, you do it no favor. Stress hormones are activated and free radicals are released, causing your cells to accelerate their aging process (and this affects not only your skin, but also organs and bones). This is a result that collides with our goals here. I do not want you to have either more stress or more free radicals in your body at the moment! So jogging in nature and joining a sports club or a gym are OK. Too much is simply too much, though, and must be avoided. Diversification is the key word here.

26. Happy Divorce

An infinite list of possibilities is left open and has to do with your personal likes and dislikes, which can help you better cope with divorce in that you breathe the air you always wanted and never did (metaphorically speaking), or do things your ex-partner did not share or did not agree for you to do on your own. **You are FREE now!** Traveling, visiting your grandparents in another state, going paragliding or jumping from a helicopter with a parachute, climbing Mount Everest, or changing religion are just a few examples. The same goes for your dislikes. If there are situations, things you have kept doing for someone else's sake, or which you find unpleasant, or boring or heavy, simply do not do them anymore. For example, you might be going to the weekly meetings at the Crochet Club, where the average age is seventy; or driving twenty miles every Monday to pick up your tennis buddy Tom and bring him back home after your matches, just because he hates driving alone. If you do not like it, do not do it! Tell him to meet you at the tennis courts and stop doing things that put you under pressure, or make you angry, or that are boring or a useless sacrifice. Make a list of your dislikes and take care of them until you have nothing to write in it anymore.

27. Happy Divorce

If you are a victim of sexual and/or mental abuse and you have already tried to give yourself a positive drive forward, but you are not able to get out of the moor, you are probably in need of counseling. Sometimes self-help works only in a further stage, when deeper wounds have healed or are in the process of healing. There are a number of social and psychological services for people in your situation, often for free. If you are thinking of divorce because of this harassment and you are afraid your ex-spouse may react violently, let the police department in your area take care of it. They will give you support in different ways, which go from referring you to help centers to opening investigations about your case. Do not be ashamed of going through these procedures. Abuse and violence, both psychological and physical, happen all social backgrounds! Especially if you have children, take courage and **say STOP THE ABUSE.**

28. Happy Divorce

Finally, you have to find balance in everything you do to be happy. Your inner peace is very important; it's the very first source of strength. Everything you perceive as disturbing must be revised, improved, changed, or simply abandoned. Do not let yourself be disturbed further! **Give your very best to help things happen in the way you like.** You also have some influence (although it's limited, as we see in a dedicated chapter) on what people think and how they act. **You cannot manipulate reality according to your likes and dislikes, but you can create it!** I hope you can understand the difference.

Aside from looking for a better future, it is fundamental that you get satisfaction from the things you have at hand. Happiness is a state of mind. It is like when you switch on a radio station you like, and it seems as if the music you hear is all about your tastes and your wishes, and your favorite song is on air! A coincidence? I wake up every morning with a smile, I wish to continue to feel happy during the day, and I let nothing and no one, not even my ex-spouse (who has given his very best), drive me up the wall for more than a very limited time (when you really can explode, if you want, and then recompose yourself and return to your old poise). This helped me tremendously to cope with my divorce and swallow all the bitter bites. Then the worst is your ex-spouse's behavior, and the happiest you can feel for finally no longer having to deal with *"such a person."* Let me tell you that my sense of inner happiness became greater every day. I was out of that insanity (my marriage). I felt like fresh water.

You know for sure that the worst part lies behind you, the bad times and the surprises. **This was the labor pain. You are now reborn and have a wonderful life before you. You are a supernova!**

PART TWO

"I Go My Way"

I Improve · I Select · I Get

ROSSANA CONDOLEO

SHIFT YOUR ENERGY, DECREASE STRESS, AND LIGHTEN THE BURDEN THAT ACCOMPANIES DIVORCE WITH IMPROVEMENTS AT HOME

Peace, like charity, begins at home.

- Franklin Delano Roosevelt (1882 - 1945)

President of the United States

An effort to improve your *four walls* and create a stress-free ecosphere is needed here.

Life is what you make it, and home is what you make it. If you want to give your life strong foundations and structure, the same applies also to your home. Your home is the place you can go back to from all the other activities (work, sports, travels, etc.), your cocoon, and you should not treat it like a dormitory. A tidy, clean, and comfortable home welcomes and takes you in its arms as you come back very tired or nervous. And since divorce is the second most serious event in the Stress Scale (following the death of the spouse) and I do not want you to go through premature aging (which is sometimes a result of heavy stress), everything around you should be pleasant and cozy. Treat your home like a part of you. We are all snails, in the end; we all need a shelter to sleep well, even the most Spartan among us. I am addressing those who live in a studio in New York as well as those who live in a farmhouse in Connecticut. The basic concept for finding harmony inside your place is the same.

You are likely to be facing a number of unpleasant situations due to divorce; therefore, what you do for your home should not be considered a further burden or duty to take care of, but a pleasure instead. If you are not interested or are too lazy—if you're too busy—to make the improvements yourself, you could hire someone to do the job for you. It is important that you do not leave someone to style your home his or her way, though. A home should mirror and look and feel like the people who live in it. And this is the reason why you may want to get rid of pieces of furniture, decorations, and other things your ex has left; memories of him or her and of your time together (good or bad). Now STOP! Ask, by written request, your ex-spouse to collect his or her personal belongings within a reasonable deadline, after which you are entitled to dispose of those things the way you deem most appropriate.

Meanwhile, you can start **putting your things in order** and throw away those tons of newspapers piled up in your living room, or you will buy a new wardrobe, so that everything will find its own place, rather than lying on the floor and/or over any available surface at your home. Chaos is creative, as long as it is limited in time and space. If you let chaos invade all of your rooms and colonize every inch of your home, the effect on your psyche will be *restlessness*. And this is what I want you to avoid. You have to be eager to go back home and sit on a comfortable couch, with cushions and a blanket.

Flowers and plants are magic in conferring your home a lively and fresh touch. They improve air quality by filtering gas pollution and helping to maintain a healthy degree of humidity. Proximity to green patches of nature will provide you also inner harmony, whether you notice it or not!

Light is very important too, as we have previously seen. Indirect light is cozy, but it must also be bright enough for your eyes not to get tired as you move about inside your home. It is advisable to use full-spectrum light bulbs, which generally have a high correlated color temperature (CCT) of 5000K – 7500K. This small trick is enough to create a much lively and natural atmosphere without interfering with your existing home lighting sets. Open your windows and always keep your curtains open so the sun can come in. Where you need privacy, you can still use light, transparent curtains, which will block indiscreet eyes but not sunlight. You need light in your life and light in your home.

What about cleanliness? As soon as their ex has closed the door behind them, some separated or divorced people begin living like wild animals in a den. The fact is that the most beautifully furnished homes will look horrible when dirtiness and messiness have taken over. If you don't intend to remain single, be aware of the fact that someone might get scared at the sight of your apartment, house or whatever, and change the idea he or she had formed about you the very first time you bring him or her home. Even if you are an Adonis with two doctorates or Jennifer Lopez in person, very interesting and interested new acquaintances could find your lifestyle so disgusting they turn around without giving you a second chance.

Personally, I cannot live in a place that is less than **pleasant and comfortable**, and beyond personal ideas of comfort and styles, there are two objective concepts that can help orient your efforts to obtain more from your home. They are harmony and space.

Harmony is an objective concept because it has been found to have more to do with mathematics and physics than with personal taste. Positioning the same things in a different way or using the same colors (think, for example, of the cushions on your coach) combined in a different way will provide a different degree of harmony. This is the reason why you need not buy new pieces of furniture or decorative objects and accessories. Not at all! You will be able to obtain more harmonious results with what you already have at hand. If you are not at all talented as an interior designer (just to use a big word; no one is really expected to be such!), you can ask for the help of a friend or a professional and be present while changes are made.

Space. You can obtain a greater sense of spaciousness even in your one-room studio apartment (where it is more needed than in a bigger home) by just repositioning your furniture so that every corner has been filled and more room is left in the middle and in the passageways. Passageways must be kept free: there is nothing more annoying than having to walk around a number of obstacles before reaching point B. Again, you may have not have noticed it yet, but this turns out to be a slight but repeated stress. Now count the times you tolerate this in a day and realize how these changes will positively reflect on your psyche.

The changes that take place must not conflict with your true inner nature. You must always feel comfortable with them. Finally, you are the king or queen of your realm, and the main objective here is for you to feel good. If you are not content with the results, please change them until you are satisfied, serene, and at peace with yourself and your home. Amen!

P.S. Do not forget to throw your used underwear in the laundry basket before leaving!

POLISHING YOUR APPEARANCE

Men in general judge more from appearances than from reality. All men have eyes, but few have the gift of penetration.

- Niccolo Machiavelli (1469 - 1527)

Writer, philosopher

Why Has Mother Nature Made Babies and Puppies So Sweet, Beautiful, and Attractive?

Before I start writing this chapter, a short introduction is due. We all would like to be loved and appreciated for what we are, regardless of our appearance. And it is also often so, at least when people are able to get to know us better. So I ask you two simple questions that will clarify why I decided (among other reasons, which I will tell you) to treat this topic. They are:

1. *Why did Mother Nature make babies and puppies so sweet, beautiful, and attractive?*

2. *Why did Mother Nature also equip with this beauty all living beings (vegetable and animal) that are dependent for their survival, reproduction, and propagation on adults of their species or other vegetable and animal forms?*

The answers are:

1. Because their beauty moves the hearts of the adults, and they will love, take care of, and protect them, so as to ensure the continuation of life.

2. Because animals and insects that have to serve them for this very same reason are lured in and do their job; think of beautiful flowers, whose vivid colors and forms attract bees and little birds who are entitled to propagate their semen.

Please, now listen carefully: **It is a cruel reality, but this means that Mother Nature knows that EVEN our own mothers and fathers have *to like* their children in order to assure them protection and nourishment!** Then, because my first commitment is to help you and only secondly to sell books and seminars, I do not want to bring you around and just ask you to ponder on this last CRUEL conclusion. Frankly, you will also not hear from me: "Wow, you look terrific with that disheveled hair! Please tell me how you get it; I want to try it too!" or "Those XXXL jeans are fantastic! What a pity they do not fit me right now! I am doing my best, but I have just reached a poor XL. Maybe in a couple of months, OK?" And so on. I also know that if the trend toward obesity is not stopped, within two decades people wearing S and M will be discriminated against for being thin.

But it is not by closing your eyes that you become really happy. It is not upon false but appealing assumptions that you should build your self-confidence. If Mother Nature does not expect your mother to be so nice as to accept her own baby, flesh of her flesh, in whatever form it comes out, why do we expect others to accept us based on our inner values—which can be the case, but is not the rule? Disillusionment follows idealization. And if you idealize society, you are more likely to suffer later on. We just have to accept things as they are and do our best to survive. **And if Mother Nature uses every kind of trick to attract love and grant life, then why should not you do the same?**

I am not a hair stylist, a dentist, or any kind of beauty operator. My objective here is not to tell you exactly what you have to do, but to call your attention to your appearance so that, if needed, you can eventually make some improvements in that direction.

Wonders Happen!

"*A couple of years ago, I used to go to the gym, and my six-pack abs were so defined that any girl would eventually touch them. Now I am more the teddy bear type!*"

"*When I was young, my silhouette was so nice and seductive that my ex had really a bad time at the beach controlling his...you know what I mean! It seems ages ago!*"

This was *me* before divorcing: "*You won't believe your eyes if you see my pictures, but I used to be a pretty nice-looking woman, up to five years ago!*"

This was *me* a few months after filing for divorce: "*Thank you, it's nice of you! I might look younger because I am happy now, and I also take better care of myself.* [Radiant smile] *Of course I look slimmer! I have lost more than* [...] (astonished reaction) *in the last few months - please don't tell anyone OK? - and dieting was no sacrifice at all. My sick marriage is behind me, and although divorce is a long and tiring process, I feel strong and can enjoy life again, old size included!*"

What I have done was set goals for my appearance (as you are suggested to do too through the Questionnaire) and start to activate myself in those directions. I found inspiration watching a TV commercial with an actress I like very much giving a testimonial. I said to myself, "If she succeeded at it, I can do it too." Visualizing your goals is really important because images, including those you build in your mind, reach the subconscious better than any words can. I am usually a disciplined person, and also very determined. It seems that as happens to many people living in unhappy marriages and facing the many side effects, I lost control of myself. I must have loved my husband very much, since he is the only one I really surrendered to. I also surrendered to him my goals as a single person and our goals as a couple, since he changed all of them to his advantage simply because they no longer fit with his own. I had to deal only with problems and chores. Alone.

THE FIRST TASK I GAVE YOU WAS TO LOOK INSIDE YOURSELF AND ESTABLISH YOUR GOALS. You never have to suffer because of, or be denatured by, another person, even someone you love. Never allow people to intrude on your life and suck your lifeblood, your enthusiasm, your

initiative—your happiness. **MOREOVER, never let someone steal your dreams. Dreams are essential for living in harmony. Without your dreams, without life goals, you get lost like a ship without a crew.** Without your dreams, you see life as gray, then black, and finally life leaves your eyes, as it happens when you are dead. And indeed you are dead. Inside.

Back to your appearance, it comes out as the sum of several factors:

1 **Self-esteem and self-confidence.**

2 **Body form** - No matter how small or tall you are, your BMI should not exceed the average for your sex and age group. Use the following link to assess your own Body Mass Index: www.cdc.gov/healthyweight/assessing/bmi/.

3 **Vitality** - This is the light you have in your eyes that says, "I love life, I love myself," and your ability to focus on people's face and eyes while talking (eye contact).

4 **Agility** - This is the result of fluid and steady movements.

5 **Tidy, unsloppy clothing** - Several tests (same person, same circumstances, different

clothing) confirm that "clothes make the monk."

6 **Well-cared-for skin, hands, and nails** - No matter what your age is, you can always look wonderful provided it is evident that you take care of your skin (it must not be yellowish or squamous, or show blemishes).

7 **Tidy, combed hair** - Experimenting has no limits, but styling and color should not be extreme if you are over fifty.

8 **Teeth** - Be proud of your smile.

I am now talking about appearance, which is what people see. What they hear, of course, and how you make yourself interesting with your social qualities, is another topic. Everyone is interesting per se! Everyone adds color to the world, and that makes it so varied and worth discovering. You have your own personality, and you do not have to change it at all if you are happy with it.

About improving one's own appearance, the **Brad Pitts and Angelina Jolies among you can skip this chapter**. For the others who may have put their appearance in the corner for a while, it is time to grab the toolbox and make some repairs!

1. Self-Esteem and Confidence

You are very fortunate if as a child, you already had a certain degree of both self-esteem and self-confidence. There are schoolboys and schoolgirls who sit in the first row, right in front of the desk, and seem to say to their teachers: *"I am as clever as you, only a little bit smaller!"* They seem to advance this way along their whole life, partly thanks to their genes, partly thanks to a social background that gave them certainties and support. As grown-up people, they vacillate less in difficult situations, such as divorce. But they are not at all vaccinated against bad surprises. **At times an excess of self-confidence can produce deeper feelings of disillusionment. The reason is simple: the qualities or features you are basing your self-confidence on are not always interesting and important for all mankind.** For example, if you are proud of your perfect body, but your ex-spouse married you because you were good at making barbecue before turning vegetarian, it's no surprise that he or she went away with his or her teddy bear-like assistant. Or if you are proud of being a very well-informed person and this, to some degree, is thanks to the fact that you engulf yourself in every edition of *The New York Times* from page 1 up to the obituaries, including the weekends, it is somewhat understandable that your ex-spouse felt you were spending too much time with the news and moved to his or her personal trainer's apartment.

There is really an infinite list of (more or less curious) features people are proud of and that make them self-assured people. This is really positive! Try to be open and eventually broaden the variety of your qualities (those that make your self-esteem grow) so that you never have to be confronted with shortages. **Intrinsic values and qualities are age-free.** For example, **social competencies or a good heart**. A good-hearted person generally goes to bed with a good feeling and wakes up with a good feeling. When egoism, resentment, and hatred do not permanently live in your heart (although it is human that they come and visit you at times), your appearance takes on a special aura, which is perceivable as soon as you enter a place.

This kind of charisma can make an elf as self-confident as a giant. I'll take the liberty of making a tribute to my Grandma Angela. She had huge social competencies and was extremely good at heart. In her small home, she used to gather all her family members, and with them all their friends. She didn't directly invite them, but these people couldn't help but come to her place, like wasps to honey, every day of the week! She was indeed not a very talkative woman. She never said a bad word or criticized, and could sacrifice all her time listening to everybody who needed to vent or to solve a problem. She was a devoted Catholic, a devoted mother, a devoted friend, sister, grandmother—everything she did, she did with devotion. In her last years, she was really tired because of all these people going in and out of her home and needing comfort or advice. She used up very big reserves of physical and mental energy this way. It was not a house, but a kindergarten, a sports club, an after work, a counseling center for everybody. And when she suddenly died at the age of sixty-seven, no one could take her place. Hundreds of people in her neighborhood felt like orphans. I miss not only her, but also those gatherings and that profusion of life. Her light, her silent warmth! She was not aggressive, not competitive, not a social climber. She was not trying to be the center and the head of such a big community, but she was, indeed. With her the community disappeared, and unfortunately, I could never enjoy the company of those people again.

Taking inspiration from people we like and respect for their special achievements can bring a lot of improvements to our life, without particular effort, because emulation is mostly an unconscious process. How this positively reflects on the external part of us—that is, our appearance—is also pretty obvious!

2. Body Shape

I find some bodies are very interesting and appealing, even in their imperfection. The fact that it is people who like people, and not magazines model agencies and beauty farms, is commonly underestimated.

Another truth is that there is always someone who finds you particularly attractive, even when you do not exactly conform to the classic definition of beauty. I have seen little people marrying normal, good-looking people and having much more romantic success than "Wow!" people. Many "Wows" have more relationship problems than people who are less equipped. But this is another problem, and it often originates in the belief that "Wows" are whimsical (which is sometimes true, at least as much as any other normal human being) or too highly positioned to approach. Thousands of different cultural groups exist on earth, each possessing its own tastes in matters of body shape. Tastes in appearance (beauty, body shape, and clothing) are also different depending on whether you live in the country or in a city. And tastes change within the same person too, so that, for example, as a woman in her forties, I prefer more fleshy and well-built men than I did in my twenties, when I preferred skinny boys.

Consequently, your weight is nothing you have to fight against if you feel perfectly happy in your size. On the other hand, it is not that easy to abstract yourself from your context. As a human being, you are also a social being (except some unlucky exceptions—*grin*!), and willing or not, you make assumptions based on the experiences you collect. After a certain amount of disappointing feedback, you will be likely to think or behave differently. The range of these reactions is great, going from light frustration to social alienation and even suicide.

If you are too much overweight or too much underweight, you may want to ask yourself if the cause lies in your broken marriage—that is, if it is the result of your unhappiness. Find a balance in your relationship and try to understand whether **you delivered your dreams into the hands of your ex husband or wife** (or shortly-to-be-ex if you are still separated), **who made no good use of them or buried all of them so that you remained without your very foundation, your spine— your dreams and projects, your own happiness (not that of your spouse or your**

children). I will confirm their importance throughout this book! If this is the case, open your heart and your mind to dreaming again (as I asked you in the first place), like a bud that suddenly blooms after a long time of frost. This is possible for all living beings. This is possible for you too. And then, every improvement, every diet, every plan, every goal, will be attainable when you dream again and you strive for your own objectives.

A point in favor of setting the goal of attaining a normal shape (without expecting to look like a sixteen-year-old, though) is that more weight invariably means more health disorders. And if you say that you are fit at double your normal weight, I believe you—up to a certain extent. Then you must compare your performance and endurance not only by participating in sporting activities, but also by regularly doing what people of normal weight do without becoming short of breath or getting arrhythmia. As weight increases, people tend to start avoiding situations like stairs (you look for lifts), short walks (you drive to get to the bakery around the corner), gardening (it was once your favorite hobby, but now your neighbor's boy is always eager to mow the grass for a couple of bucks!), etc. And due to the stress that too much body weight places on muscles and bones, you become more prone to injuries such as joint dislocations and muscle strains, which alter and slow down the rhythm of your daily life. In the long run, obesity can affect organs and their functions, so chronic diseases may occur—for example, diabetes, heart disease, and stroke. Finally, it is not only a question of how attractive and appealing you can be. Normalizing your weight makes you healthier and more active. Being overweight means carrying a basket with a certain load (visualize your weight in terms of butter barrels!). The heavier the basket, the more tired you feel. You can tell me that it is still OK, but I bet it is not a good feeling after all!

3. Vitality

Vitality is much more a product of mental fitness than of physical exercise. A whippy, springy, agile person might indeed not always be able to embody the concept of vitality if happiness does not flow inside that person and permeate his or her sins. BEING ACTIVE and REACTIVE—this is vitality. **Happiness, as we have seen, goes hand in hand with dreams and love**; the love you give (imbalance brings you to sanctity, but not necessarily to happiness) and take (you cannot serve only yourself and be satisfied; apart from its being immoral and unethical, there will be a time when other parties understand your egoistic game and simply close the tap). The value you give to the things you have at hand makes you vital; if you give them no value, then you are not able to enjoy and absorb their positive energy. **Vitality has to do with the meaning of your actions in a universal sense, not subjectively** (some find it particularly meaningful to sit on the couch twenty-four hours a day and play with their PlayStation). Mindfulness and spirituality are important too. Only emotions, the good ones, can light your eyes in that special way that makes the entire world love you at first sight.

4. Physical Agility

Anyone, at any age, can become agile with a little exercise at the gym, at home, or within nature. The aim is unlocking muscles and ligaments to facilitate body movements.

It is not something you really need. It is nice that everyone has his or her typical gait. Should your movements look awkward, there is something extra you can do to add charm to your appearance. *Posture management courses* (for those with skeletal problems) and *modeling courses* (for those with sedentary jobs such as truck drivers, PC operators, etc.) work, and they're fun. In my opinion, it is enough to go for a thirty-minute walk with fifteen minutes of bending exercises at home, twice a week. Using video training is also an option; there are hundreds of DVDs available to make the choice hard (follow your taste; you have to enjoy what you do!), along with thousands free videos that can be downloaded from YouTube and other sites.

5. Clothing

It is sad, I know! But as previously mentioned, people react differently to good or sloppy clothing. The good news is that good clothes are available to everybody at affordable prices, and even those who do not consider it a priority to improve their look might give it a try. You could ask a fashion-forward friend to go shopping with you so that you do not buy something that will later make you uneasy, since new outfits do not suit your personality. Let me explain: if you are the *casual* type, for example, there are a lot of ways to improve your casual wear. When comfortable clothing is a must, you can work on color combinations, fabrics, styles, and details that enhance your figure and conceal problem areas (if any). The right size is also important. Clothing must be neither too tight nor too large—that is, you should wear exactly your size, with a maximum of one size larger and never a size smaller.

You do not have to wear labels or the latest collection of designer clothes (if you have the money, why not?) to have a pleasant look. "No-name" fashion industries make quality clothing too, and apart from making six hours queue for the sales of (again) "big designer", you can look for online sales. You just need to sign up at the websites of your favorite online shops or big department stores who have a web presence. Then you can save time and get at home what you would normally find after hours of shopping trips. I shop online, and I find it as fun, or even more fun, than shopping in person.

For shopaholics I have no suggestions. They always stay up to date on latest trends and bargains to get labels, or quality, or both (grin!) at the best prices.

My cheeks turn red now. Due to pre-, during-, and post-traumatic divorce syndrome, or because they never personally took care of their laundry before, some forget about the meaning of "tidy" and "clean." If you want to wear the same shirt for two days, it is up to you, but it brings no improvement to your appearance and social life. People might start to be critical after a while (to use a euphemism), and if it is your boss, well...it is not that good at all! The last thing you need now is to be pointed out as "the stinker."

Sorry if I insist, but I think that some people do not have as good a chance as others on dating websites just because it's apparent that they are sloppy and untidy. Think about this: *speed dating* works on the principle that people establish a connection in the first few seconds they *see* each other. Then they can support their first assessment within seven minutes by asking questions. Women in particular are very picky about this. Before you leave this section saying "Nonsense," please ask yourself if your look needs to be revised a little bit.

6. Skin, Hands, Nails

This is no longer (hallelujah!) a "for women only" territory. More and more men regularly visit beauty centers and let their skin (wealth of hair included), hands, and nails be cared for. Thanks to modern cosmetics, it is possible to address and improve any features that may be deemed not esthetic. Again, you can argue that esthetics finds no universal definition. For example, more and more people love tattoos, piercings, and so on, and think they are the most appealing features on their bodies. Others react with rejection. Apart from this specific example, there are things that everyone has that can be treated, removed, or improved (like hair, spots, scales, etc.) because it is almost universally accepted that smooth skin is an appealing quality. Unfortunately, after puberty nobody looks like a newborn baby, and the majority are busy with hair removals, cream spreading, wellness baths, and so on. There are affordable new small electric appliances that have completely replaced big and expensive laser equipment, once available only to specialized beauty and medical centers, which let you remove your hair permanently and painlessly at home.

Since I suffer from MCS (multi chemical sensitivity), I invent non-toxic recipes and manufacture myself many of my personal care, cosmetic, and household cleaning products. I use natural ingredients such as bio oils and fruit acids, and I am convinced that "do-it-yourself" is a valid alternative to industrially manufactured products, especially if you think about the exorbitant prices in the anti-aging segment.

About the new trend in hand makeup and nail design and styling, a new fashion industry is booming. I had a neighbor a couple of years ago who was a nail stylist, and she owned a sports cabriolet as well as several furs and designer dresses; she also lived in the same building as I, in one of the most renowned districts of the capital city. I think I will have my daughter consider following this professional route instead of wasting decades on books and never being able to buy such a car!

Now, if hands and nails have grown so much in importance as to become a worldwide fetish, you would want to follow the trend, and although you might not wear fake nails or use nail polish (for men this would be not appropriate, I think!), you might try to do your best to keep your nails in order. Many people have reported to me how disturbed they were at the sight and touch of a new partner's hands. Hands play a big role in intimate contact, and rough, dirty, black-nailed hands (to picture the worst possibilities) are simply disgusting.

Finally, every age is nice and important and brings with it something special, from zero to a hundred years and more. We all get old; we had better accept it rather than make it a lifelong problem. Anyway, aging does not mean you must let go. My mother, who is nearly seventy, has never put her nose out the door without perfect makeup and hair styling. My grandfather is 104 years old, and he still uses spray men's perfumes after his morning toilet. I admire people who have such respect for themselves and for others—who are not required to love them just because of their inner qualities—that they try, within their means, to be neat and well groomed.

7. Hair

Haircut, hairstyle, and hair hygiene account for more than 30 percent of our appearance, on average, and on certain occasions (social events) even 50 percent. Hair stylists possess magic powers; they can turn a Cinderella into a princess by just taking care of her hair. This is also the most convenient way to add value to your appearance. Some might also lose hair as a consequence of the stress of divorce; in these cases you should ask your hairdresser to treat it more gently than ever.

Most women close unpleasant chapters in their lives by changing color and haircuts. This is also a way to cut their past and say: *"I am a new person starting a new life."* I find it a good idea, provided you do not exaggerate the use of colors as if you were a parrot, especially if you are over fifty.

8. Teeth

One of the first things I did while taking care of my appearance after filing for divorce was go to a dentist and let him work on my old fillings and small caries. I can proudly smile and breathe close to people without having to put a hand in front of my mouth. Just joking—my situation was not so dramatic!

Back to you: if dental treatments can sometimes be expensive, depending on your health insurance, hygiene is not. Some tooth-pastes that promise to whiten your teeth work quite well; those that remineralize your tooth enamel have a plus. Tooth whitening through bleaching generally produces fantastic results and lets your face really shine; if you are used to drinking five cups of coffee a day, or drink red wine, or smoke, the effects will not be lasting, though.

There are a number of other cosmetic solutions to improve your smile. Again, if your financial means are not very high, look on the Internet for sites where health care treatments are affordably auctioned (and they range from internal medicine to breast surgery up to teeth bleaching). You describe what sort of treatment you are looking for, and practitioners and health care specialists of all sorts will offer their services at a given price. Since quality is also an important criterion, look at reviews first.

A HDP's Charisma

Well-groomed is the keyword. If you look good (not cute in the sense of Mr. and Mrs. Perfect Nose-Butt-Or-Whatever; everyone, really everyone, can look good!) and well groomed even in the most difficult circumstances, you will be proud of yourself because it means you let no one and nothing KO you. Of course, you also have the substance to shine like that; your appearance is the product of what you are inside, as we have seen. You are self-confident, open, strong, reactive, receptive, and social.

I am not willing to bring this chapter about appearance much further (talking about esthetic surgery, for example). My first duty here is to call your attention to facts and improvements that most coaches prefer to ignore in favor of more metaphysical and spiritual values.

"**Eyes are the mirror of the soul.**" We have seen how important is to look into people's eyes and communicate a feeling of vitality, self-confidence, and availability. **But appearance is also the mirror of your soul, and this also**

works! You will reinforce the idea that you are doing fine (in your subconscious and in the outer world) as long as you maintain a well-groomed appearance and let no one know that you have problems at home. Your new life is also made of exterior improvements (if needed!), which do not follow, but come together with, those that take place deep inside you.

HOW TO WIN SOCIAL NETWORKS AND PUBLIC OPINION CHALLENGES

*There are certain times when public opinion
is the worst of all opinions.*

- Sébastien-Roch-Nicolas Chamfort (1741 - 1794)

Writer

Is there anything more volatile than public opinion? Think about it. If your answer is no, then why do most people care so much about people's opinion?

Public opinion can be the opinion of the citizens of a country (a great number of people); or the opinion of the inhabitants of your small village in Utah or Pennsylvania. I generally use this term to define what the people you associate with think of you.

Public opinion can rapidly change; the advertising industry, PR agencies, etc., make huge profits exploiting this fact. Another fact is that researchers work every day to understand how this is possible and why **people change their minds so fast, even upon apparently non-evident or at times totally false information**.

Too many factors influence people's opinion, and those wanting to take advantage of this fact must use different strategies based on age, sex, interests, and various other parameters to *manipulate* public opinion in a particular segment. Now, think of presidential campaigns, and how they are strategically played through blogs and digital social networks! Facebook, Twitter, and so on have added complexity to the the picture. New important factors that influence public opinion have risen; for example, how many friends or followers an entity (person, group, or business) can count on or how many likes this entity accumulated. Everyone seems to be urged to perform on a social stage and show they can have so many followers too. This causes many to live more publicly than they are willing to. They *must* write something, and occasionally, this something will change the opinion of the followers to the point that many will leave/unfollow. So easy is it in social networks when you no longer want to follow someone you just click *remove*, and that person disappears from your screen and from your life. Then it happens that after the first bad experience, many will opt for a less intense life and presence on social media, while others will become Mr. and Mrs. Perfect: they will display only good-looking pictures and publish only short, meaningful, and well-thought-out comments. Not a bad idea, in the end! We will see why later on.

I also like people who really do not care what they unveil; they are genuine and behave and write with spontaneity; *they accept the consequences: life is a show!*

Businesses and groups respond to public opinion not much differently from private entities. If you are running a company or a group in a social network, you may be likely to influence, with your personal image, the image of your social entities, especially if you bring your private life into their midst. A divorce is a container of financial, family, private, sexual, legal, social, and emotional issues. A divorce can trigger so much negative power to deeply change your inner nature—a real bomb in your life! Some become full of hatred, resentment, and rage. Others react by becoming ice cold and ignoring the needs of their families. You are now learning how to channel this gigantic explosive energy into your goals and so doing, converting it into positive results. As a human being, though, you can fail. Then you need to contain the consequences.

Now, please decide whether you are interested in having or creating and maintaining a good public opinion/image, or if you REALLY do not give a damn (sorry for being so blunt) about what people think or say. Then act accordingly! You are now going through a very special time when your expectations are higher than ever concerning your social life, and by unveiling your thoughts, difficulties, and fears, or telling people about how you KOed your ex in front of your friends or on digital networks, you could generate enormous waves of love in your direction—but also annoyed reactions. People do not like to hear or read over and over again how sad or bad you are because of your divorce. They want to hear how well you are doing despite divorce. They want to hear that you are strong and much happier than before, since now you are free like a bird!

The first time you publish a picture of you fictionally hanging from the ceiling of your bathroom, your followers will find it very funny and will comment: *"Hey dude...head up...Go and use that rope to tie up a new someone instead!"* By the second time you publish something like that, they will comment: *"Hey dude...still hanging there? What about a beer at the pub at 08:00 p.m.?"* The third time you will find almost no comments except *"Hey, how are you doing? Would you come and join the 4Ds Group* (which stands for Desperate and Depressed Divorced Dudes)? *We are always looking for people like you!"*

The most rapid and effective way to overcome adversity is to count on yourself, to activate and use your own resources. Fortunately they are infinite, like the universe.

This is really the first and last chapter in which I will allow myself to be somewhat cynical. But I am doing it with the aim of preventing spiritually expensive disillusionments. Perhaps you have already come to the same conclusion!

After high school and college, when you shared even your panties with your best friends (to use a metaphor), the time that follows is mostly characterized by what I call "social theater." It *seems* everyone is nice and eager to befriend. You go out with those people, exchange work information, put your hands on each other's shoulders, and *seem* to be the closest people in the world. But then, right when you really need some help and ask for a little effort in your direction, you notice how **superficial** most of these so-called "friendships" are (a few of them are true, though).

Another feature of this social theater is that everybody is perfect; they do not know what fear is and have no problems in the world; and this should be your attitude from now on. Everything is OK! *"How do you do?"* *"Fine, thanks!"* Wow...I meet only happy people, I think, every time! A couple of days later, though, I hear rumors of them being divorced, or fighting against cancer in the last stage, or living through some other dramas they faced alone or strictly within their family. I think my generation (I was born in the late sixties) has learned to cope alone with their problems by maintaining a brilliant cover of perfection. We have grown up watching TV commercials. That's it! Those who used to show up as whiny will always be considered as such. There are no categories in the middle: you are either a winner or a loser.

It is a very difficult issue. On the one hand, you now need more love and understanding than ever. On the other hand, you must grow stronger and even show the world that you are doing better than ever. There is always, always a good side of the coin, and in this case, there are even two!

First, the time you feel socially discomforted is short, and goes from the day you file for divorce up to the day you realize you have a stand-alone life. This gap time can be sad sometimes because your interpretation of social interaction is filtered through your bigger need of social confirmation. Since as a newly separated or divorced person you are mourning over your other half, you need some time for your mind to extend, stretch, enlarge, and develop to the point where you have built the second missing half, and you are again an independent, **Whole, One**. It is a very natural process that takes place in all those who have not divorced because they have previously found a new lover. All the others will more or less consciously go through this phase and feel, at the end of it that they are better able to make progress as a single person than as a couple because:

1. They look for the people who are interesting to them and not to their partners.

2. They will instinctively find people who are in a similar situation (thanks to the mechanisms that I have explained

previously in the example of the *Job in Paris*).

3. They are radiant in their approach, so positive and attractive with their rejuvenated new spirit and personality, that people cannot but respond positively.

So never mind! Make an initial effort and you will see results that you will be proud of.

Ok, now a little bit more acid talking against *"look how I feel bad right now."* Generally speaking, there are a lot of people who feel and act competitively. They cannot be other than that. It is in their DNA! These people, who can be everywhere around you (in your family, at work, at your sports club, among your old friends, etc.), might even enjoy your difficulty. They might come to the point of using information or your state of mind to their advantage against you, and the least that can happen is that you feel even poorer than before when you go and confide in them. Envy, jealousy, and (again) competition have always existed, from the dawn of mankind. Romulus and Remus, and Cain and Abel are examples. Entire dynasties have been exterminated under illicit feelings and the offenses of their own members. Today the "snaking and malignant feelings" are the same, only their ways are different.

Many of you—as well as I—live far away from their birthplace and their original family, and old friends are scattered all over the world. In this case, should you absolutely need a shoulder, it is advisable to get in touch with them (via the Internet) rather than open your heart to people you know but never had to share your bread with before. You never know how and where they will report your story. On the other hand, there are those who have made a mission of helping people in difficult or critical situations and are really eager to listen to and support you. Sometimes you do not even have to pay a penny; anonymous self-aided centers and groups, online forums, social services, and counseling offered by religious groups locally do a good job and, with few exceptions, do not release your private life to the daily news.

In principle, the concept is: you share beauty and happiness, not problems. Then, your child's 104° F fever becomes "a bit of temperature." Your dismissal is sold as "sabbatical time." Your divorce is a "nice trip to a new world"! And do you know what? You are indeed able to transform divorce into new life.

No one can help you except yourself, since you know better than anyone what you want. Consequently, as far as you can cope alone with everything, do it. Unpleasant situations, if any, will end—a further point in favor of being secretive about eventual negative feelings!

Mother Nature has given you all that you need—strength, flexibility, creativity, good will, perseverance, open heart, harmony, and the beauty of positive thoughts. It is more than you need to get out of the mist and be proud of your own means, resources, and results. Be thankful for what you already have and focus on the objectives you have written on your Vision board. They are easily reachable if you just forget of your past. Enjoy your present and make every moment a precious one. Put your internal harmony and happiness against your divorce challenges. Every day is made of twenty-four hours, and each hour is made of a thousand moments. As I previously told you, you can allow yourself short times of sadness or anger, even in the most explosive ways. I really do not expect you to play Superman or Wonder Woman, and there are situations and events connected to divorce that really make a saint touch the hell ground, especially when you have Satan as an ex. Think of my words and wait a second before tweeting or writing on Facebook against your ex or your lawyers, whoever or whatever. Calm down. Tomorrow you will certainly appraise your situation differently. Personally, I need time to digest a new bitter bite. For very bad ones, I even allow myself two days (do not laugh; it is true!). But really no longer than that! We are made so perfect that we can set our mind to face any situation. We are so adaptive that if needed, we can survive a long time in the most unthinkable situations. Again, it is only a matter of how you react and how you think of a problem. The problems are real, but also real are their solutions.

It is always advantageous to maintain a positive image outside. This will be rewarding on a professional level too, since career people are asked not to bring personal problems to work. Particularly if you are striving and competing for career advancement, it is advisable to make no one apart of what you are living at home. Colleagues can transform into opponents the next day, and everything you say can be used against you. Men automatically become "losers," and women become "desperate." Notwithstanding the high rate of divorce, society goes on penalizing those involved. It is a dog chasing its tail, since no marriage is safe, UNFORTUNATELY!

If you are a little good looking, there is a chance your friends, or at least some of them, will start looking at you as a potential "husband or wife stealer." So try to be patient and avoid situations that could appear to confirm these fears.

You will be banned from certain friends' family gatherings. They will either think you would suffer by sitting among happy families, or that you are just so negatively charged at the time and in such a bad mood that you may cause their children to cry, their soufflé to fall, their grass to turn yellow, and who knows what else. It is a joke, but please understand that there will be some changes. Some will be surprisingly positive, pleasant, or funny, like being invited by your best friends to blind-date dinners with their single colleagues, or receiving sympathy calls from people you had never expected to be so kind. Many of these people are really good willed. Others will just be putting a good face on a bad game and are perhaps dreaming of occupying your beautifully furnished ocean-view villa with tropical garden as soon as you are no longer able to pay the rent or mortgage. This will remain only a dream of theirs as long as you like it and want to live there!

In publicly announcing your divorce (which is not at all compulsory), use the fewest words possible. It is also advisable (learn to put a leash on your tongue if needed) to use the fewest words possible in answering private or very private questions, such as those about possessions or your sex life. Privacy is a plushy, soft blanket that makes you feel comfortable, as opposed to the freezing Public. It happens to me all over again when I speak too much: I first feel relieved because I have shared something painful or disturbing or both. Then I start to feel naked, so much that I promise myself to send my tongue to the CIA for it to learn how to keep secrets once for all!

Back to the pressure that digital social networks put on you: please do not feel any. No pressure at all! The Internet has changed the way we socialize and compensates for our lack of physical socialization. It gives you the impression of a friendly, open world, which is fairly true as long as this closeness remains digital. Do you think Shakira would like her 70,390,386 (this is the updated number of her Facebook fans) to visit her at home and say *good night* personally? Do you think Jude Law would be happy to invite for dinner, let's say a small part of his hungry (and not for food) female Facebook fans? I have in my friends list a couple of people I never met in my life, with whom I can talk, but I do not even know what they do for a living! What if they work at the Pizza Connection? I just ignore it! Why the heck must I tell them how I feel when my ex comes and puts me down? It's very different when you are in a group that shares the same interests, hobbies, or experiences. And even there, you will always meet impolite, hypercritical, rejectful people who seem to have a life only on the Internet and grow old before their PC screens just like in the movie *Surrogates* starring Bruce Willis. These singular people, who thanks to the huge number of their comments are well situated in the community rank, usually do not read carefully what you write; they are just interested in posting a comment and gaining visibility. You will find that there is very little correspondence between your news and these comments, but it is not important, is it? And this happens also when they report what you have said or written to the others, in their own words: it has nothing to do with the information you have given. It does really matter, doesn't it? Or does it?

Think about this: you can better control one piece of information than ten. And one hundred better than one thousand. Fewer details are always much better than lot of details. Things remain on the Internet for decades; they will be haunting you your life long! It is all about your life. It is all about you. And you are the most important person in the world for yourself right now. Have respect for your person, and the others will respect you as a result. Provide all the people you want with warmth and love, and be a great giver, both in the physical and in the digital world. But please do not use social networks like a Wailing Wall. You probably perceive, at this point, that something is moving positively in your life right now. And tomorrow, and the day after tomorrow, and next week, it will be a lot better. This sorrow, if any, is disappearing like snow in the sun. Just stick to your dreams, think of them, activate your life energy, and forget about your past—ignore it. That belongs to another life, to another person. As I told you before, your cells are replaced, and every new cell will receive your new positive energy and will react accordingly.

Try to identify "buds" among your friends— i.e., divorced or divorcing energetic and positive people or singles. With them you can enjoy life more than with married people right now. I am not saying that you have to exclude yourself from the company of other people's husbands and wives. But many of them may find it difficult to share your return to party life. You want to have fun again, so gather fun people around you.

Social Homework

VIPs usually have personal counselors, assistants, and bodyguards (especially these!) who make their lives easier while divorcing. You have to help yourself. And the next thing is a homework assignment I would like you to do: go to all your social networks and web pages and the forums where you have a membership, and write *"I am happy!"* This is the seed of your Happiness Tree. It will grow bigger every day until it is so bright and high that the Happiness Tree will protect you and offer you shelter. After that, virtually give it water every day, writing a short, positive sentence or affirmation about why you feel happy, for example: *"Today I am happy because I was able to finish a half hour early at work and was able to use this time to go visit my old uncle Ted, whom I have not seen in ages."* It can come from observing nature: *"How nice! I saw a squirrel today in the park burying an acorn in the ground for the winter,"* or *"Snowflakes on my cheeks have made my Sunday morning!"* or the good things that are NOW in your life and that no one can take away from you, such as: *"I was so happy yesterday baking chocolate muffins with my little girl!"* It can also be something that has to do with your inner values, or other people's: *"A beautiful brunette with striking eyes has invited me for coffee on Saturday. Let's see what it brings!"* OK, now really inner: *"I feel good when I can donate something of myself, be it physical or spiritual."* That's better, though somewhat ambiguous! Or simply a positive observation of something that happened to you that day for which you may be grateful: *"My boss called me into his office today and handed over two— repeat, two—of his biggest clients to me. And it's not even Christmas time!"*

Every time you meet one of your friends—and this is a part of your homework too—do the same: tell him or her that you are happy for something. Before going to sleep, look at your dreams list or vision board and go to bed with a smile. **In a couple of weeks, your friends will start complimenting you on the brilliant new light in your eyes and your lively, positive attitude. And you know what? They are right!**

PS. "A single rose can be my garden...a single friend, my world." - **Felice Leonardo "Leo" Buscaglia Ph.D. (1924 - 1998)**

DAILY BREAD, OR THE SCIENCE OF DOING THE JOB YOU LIKE

Chose a job you love, and you will never have to work a day in your life.

- Confucius (551 - 479 B.C.)

Teacher, philosopher, writer, politician

Work is a very significant part of our life; this is also known among ants.

Whether work occupies a very significant part of our life is something that very much depends on what we do for a living and how we master our time.

Whether work occupies a very significant part of our thoughts very much depends on our dedication to it and how much we like it.

Now, if you have truly answered your questionnaire, you have now on your Vision board or document something that should more or less precisely describe your job. I am sure you have been pondering your answer much longer than the other questions. Here the social conditionings are very strong, and we learn already at primary school, that becoming a doctor brings more money than becoming a fireman.

In my opinion, nowadays still **one third of all people are engaged in work activities that follow their mom's and dad's "orientation,"** desires, and wants. And whether this influence was direct or hidden so deeply as to be almost subliminal is not relevant. One third of active people on the job market are simply performing and are not dedicated.

Another **one third are engaged in jobs they accepted because they were not in a position to choose.** They simply needed to take the first job available, which alone, or together with other two or three other small jobs, pays the bills at the end of each month, every year, their whole life long.

Then **only one third of all people do what they like most, following their dreams**. And since dreams can change, changing jobs can be a consequence.

Young people, while at school, are very influenced by teachers. Taking the best notes in math does not mean that my vocation is doing calculations; I am just good at it. I have a talent, but there are young people who are multi-talented (I was one of them), and in this case it is difficult to find an orientation. Therefore, what is the most valid principle that will surely bring you to success and happiness in the work arena? Yes, exactly what Confucius a couple of years ago said: **you must like it**! So simple the truth is! And I am firmly convinced that the simplest thing can teach us the deepest meanings of life.

Now, in a number of cases a divorce brings about job changes. Reasons can be:

1. You have moved from somewhere in the world to follow your ex, and now you find no reason to continue to live there.

2. You have to earn more now that you have to pay the rent and the bills alone, and your present job just covers half of your monthly costs.

A **divorce can be compared to (re)-birth—both have love and pain behind them**. You feel you cannot stand your actual job anymore, and you need to do something more meaningful and pleasing to your true Self.

Please try to analyze your personal situation now, and if you are content with it, you have to make no changes at all. While divorcing, we connect more to other people than ever before (looking for love, security, a gravity center, confirmations, new possibilities, and so on), and if you have been working for a long time at the same workplace, some colleagues might have become friends; it can be sort of stabilizing to continue working at the same place, since you know that *you belong* there. And if they are real friends, you will keep in touch if you change jobs.

Back to **"I must like my job,"** which represents the essence of this chapter. **When we do something we like, we are not only happy. We are also very strong!** You are so motivated and so determined that you can overcome any difficulty. You can take on double or thrice the workload of people who just do their jobs for a living. You have much more initiative, and you have a lot more chances to make a career or invent something great as an entrepreneur when you do something you like. You will keep motivated, and your satisfaction at work will be double that of people who are at the wrong workplace because you simply need less to achieve more. You are already positively charged on your own.

When you do something you like, your mind still works by night, producing wonderful new ideas in every aspect of your job. So if you own a company, for example, you can wake up with a new product idea, or a new way to merchandise it, or the feeling that your assistant is not trustworthy and you must start investigating that. It is amazing how well you can run your activities when you like your job. The quality, the efficiency, and the creativity you produce is above average because the average is given by the one third of the people who work for a living (we all work for a living, but I am sure you understand what I mean!) and the one third of the people who "were brought" to do what they do. And, again, if mathematics is not an opinion, you possess the best chances to be successful in your job and VERY VERY HAPPY!

The one third of the people who work for a living do not probably know that by doing so, they will hardly move upward on their development ladder. They will come back home very frustrated, like those who do their job because it was the dream of their parents. Frustration is a big problem in any relationship, and it triggers the worst health troubles. These people may have no problems with bringing their jobs home because they try to forget about it as soon as their eight hours are over. Then they place a good amount of their missed satisfaction in other activities, hobbies, and interests, which compensate for their hunger for joy and creativity, or action (when their jobs are too routine, for example). Yes, but we know that when we do not directly satisfy basic needs, imbalance is always the result. Feeding with surrogates is not a good alternative, especially in the long run.

What I wanted to do as an adult was already clear to me when I was eleven years old. I chose a high school that gave me the basics for later attending my college. At my college more than 50 percent of the students left between the first and the second year; it was really hard to pass an examination there. I graduated in three years, while my course of studies normally lasts four years and more. I was a party geek too. I always had my dream before me, so I proceeded like a tank, focusing on my target and seeing no obstacles, only challenges. I had a plan, and I was so resolute that I could study even under the most difficult circumstances. I had a dream, and it was very much in conflict with my mother's dream. She wanted me to become a gynecologist! She had brainwashed me for a long time. She also wanted to choose my college. She challenged me in order to make me capitulate, and I had to fight hard to go to that college, to take that course of studies. But I won. My mother wanted my sister to become an engineer, and indeed she induced my sister to enroll in engineering! My sister left engineering two years later, after passing some very difficult examinations. Nonetheless, she felt really exhausted and demotivated; her dream was graduating from the sports academy. And she got her graduation—with honors!

When you do something you do not like, be it in your personal life or in your job sphere, it comes out sooner or later. Perhaps it was also the case with your marriage and the person you chose as your spouse.

The number of performances and competencies required by most job positions on the market would imply three people doing the job. But indeed, only one person is employed. You cannot really let your psyche and your body undergo such a pressure (most illnesses have a psychosomatic matrix) without the needed motivation and determination. These are not always acquired on demand—for example, through motivational training. You must be strong from the very beginning.

You must be able to say: "I love my job!" and feel your heart full of joy. And you really do not mind if it is Monday or Friday, since you like each and every weekday.

"Chose a job you love, and you will never have to work a day in your life," **by Confucius**, is really a pearl of wisdom. Every job, be it mining or deep sea fishing, for example, becomes light and pleasant and not perceived as a job when you like it.

In connection with fashion shows, there is so much to do on a commercial, organizational, and financial level that designers usually cannot get enough sleep. And yet they consider themselves artists, the concept of artist evoking more a bohemian character than someone who has an agenda full of business duties. They are so happy and dedicated that they perceive their jobs as a joy, a source of life and energy without which they could not live.

Therefore, while two thirds of the active people lose their energy behind their unloved jobs (and are subject to stress disorders), one third of them take energy from their loved jobs. It is this last one third who normally move the lines in the world economy. I do not have to make a list. Think about the biographies of most known rich people, and you will find confirmation of that.

Now, if you belong to the one third who are happy with their jobs, and you can confirm this even when your boss does not hear you, then I hope you KEEP IT UP! Should you not, you might want to review your situation now, be it before, during, or after the divorce. As already pointed out, you are going through a very critical time, when everything is possible and realizable.

This is true at every age of your life, though. You can always decide about tomorrow. It is important not to ignore, when the need exists, that you have to contact your inner self and let it talk to you. Let yourself be guided by your inner voice. It can be a dream, or a vision, or a piece of an idea. Put yourself in motion as soon you receive a message from your Self, even when you do not understand yet, or at least not completely, how this can be possible. Most times our subconscious knows exactly what is best for us and has already planned a sequence of actions in that direction. Sometimes you just have to start putting an idea into action, and then everything follows as a natural consequence. This happens when you work under the light of your dreams.

For those who are not eager to take risks, there is still something you can do! If you do not like your job very much, but you think that you have other priorities than looking for a new one right now, you can improve your situation at work. **Do you hate routine? Add variety! Do you hate variety and surprise? Add routine!** Let's look at a couple of examples.

If you are the kind of person who does not like routine, and a big part of your work is indeed repetitive, you can add variety and color by, for example, dividing your work into segments, and between these you introduce something new. This something new may or may not have to do with your work. What is important is that you create blocks of routine and breaks. Ask your supervisor if he or she can help you add variety to your tasks, or if you can try to cover another position.

If you have a job that's too challenging, and you meet every surprise and change with stress (instead of being thrilled), then you can try to better plan your tasks so that there is less room for unknown factors. Preventing is better than treating. You can ask your supervisor if he or she can do something to help you lessen the stress in your job. Perhaps it's not apparent that you are having trouble. If you don't provide your supervisor with feedback, he or she will assume you are doing great!

Again, we can dream and desire what we want, but if we do not help by activating our resources, then the chances that something can change for the better are really low.

Rossana Condoleo

HOW TO HANDLE YOUR EX, HIS FAMILY, AND HIS FRIENDS

Once the realization is accepted that even between the closest human beings infinite distances continue, a wonderful living side by side can grow, if they succeed in loving the distance between them which makes it possible for each to see the other whole against the sky.

- Rainer Maria Rilke (1875 - 1926)

Poet, Novelist

You are strong with your own inner happiness and with your engagement in the direction of your goals. What you have started by filling out the Questionnaire is your Life, and not the one you have had with your ex. And this is the reason why, whenever you regard your ex as past, **you are able to visualize him or her on a street, behind your shoulders, as he or she stops and you walk on farther**. You are not required to work out your marriage failures and re-experience the entire painful process of how you came to divorce. This no longer has any use! A decision has been made, by you or your partner. Now you have to look further.

You have seen how light and bright your life can be if you start dreaming again, or if you never stopped, you just go on your own way without having to compromise any longer.

If you are still separated and in the process of divorcing, with your ex-partner challenging you and making your life impossible due to possessions and children, it is even more important that you let your emotions not get the better of you all the time. Never get caught in the net of devoting all your thoughts to your troubles. You have to remain focused on your life, not the horror of these days, if any. Focus on what you want for yourself and for your children (if any) and never let your ex-ghost behind you. If your husband or your wife was not a saint during your marriage, the chances that he or she will surprise you with a nice adieu, will stay at zero. Divorce helps the true nature of everybody to come out and then endows it with a certain degree of volcanic power.

I am repeatedly told that divorce rarely runs smoothly. There are special divorce cases in which one needs all one's nerves and all my advice not to go insane. Mine was a special case! Again, the shorter a time you give to *utter frustration, rage, and so on,* the better you do for yourself and the people who live with and around you. There are indeed too many interests in the game—feelings, children, finances—and some use every means to cheat the ex. Anyway, notwithstanding the many different constellations in the divorce firmament (depending on the original union, culture, reasons to part, financial means, presence or absence of children, and so on), I can simplify and extract a couple of rules that can help to cope with ex, his family, and his friends, without pretending to provide universal solutions.

1. **Put distance between you and your ex.**

2. **Put distance between you and the family of your ex.**

3. **Put distance between you and the friends of your ex.**

People belonging to your ex's side (or front line!) who loved you before your separation will continue to do so, although your contacts may decline with time. At the beginning you should give these people time to equalize their reactions. Trying to get any kind of support from them is not a good idea. Even if the divorce is not your fault, if it is not your choice but a consequence of your ex's behavior, his or her people will be always loyal to him or her (exceptions are possible but not the rule). Should your ex disappear with your money or betray you with someone else, the other person can eventually say that you are to blame. He or she might say, *"Why did you trust him (or her)?"; "Why did you marry him (or) her?"; "You were not such a good/attractive/understanding/providing/loving partner!"* Or equally: *"You are both to blame!"* this last being an old, common one. They almost inevitably back their child, cousin, best friend, etc. and let you feel like a jerk. Limit your expectations and let time go by. They are all human beings, and the majority do not know how to handle the new situation with you. You will have always time later on, when everything has calmed down, to try to reconnect with these people, especially if there are children involved, who usually build bridges between families.

One of the most topical questions is: *"Is it a good idea to ask for help and involve his or her parents, relatives, or friends in my divorce crisis?"* My answer is: *"It is not!"* They will be thankful if you save them the trouble of having to take a position or partake in your fights. My father- and mother-in-law did not say a single word; they simply ignored our divorce as far as I was concerned, and I did not want to break their peaceful world by telling them what they did not want to know or hear. What do you want to obtain that you cannot obtain alone or with the help of professionals or people on your side (YOUR family, YOUR friends)?

I do not know how long have you been married, but surely you had to compromise a number of times about what kind of people you had at dinner or under your beach umbrella on vacation. I mean, there are really lots of your ex's connections with whom you *previously* had nothing personal to share. Now the link to them is even thinner, so that it must not be so bad to forget about them. Should you find your divorce painful because of the large number of people disappearing from your life, please reconsider the situation under a less romantic view—that is, ask yourself how important, in reality, these people are to you. Do they deserve your mourning?

Finally, think of your life as a series of opportunities. When one is over, there is another waiting for you. You now have more time to spend with YOUR FRIENDS, YOUR SIBLINGS, YOUR COLLEAGUES, and more time to make new acquaintances, which are important for your future love relationships.

If you cannot speak but bark all the time with your ex, since air is burning between you, distance is really a must. Again, in the future you will be able to make adjustments and improvements when the hard times are over.

Even couples who do not suffer from communication disorders will only take advantage of breaking up for a certain time. It is very nice to wish to maintain a good relationship to your ex, and surely you also will be able to. But this is a special time of CREATION for you, and you have to realize that life continues without him or her. Even when one of the two spouses still depends financially on the ex for a while, the financially dependent partner must not be subjugated or controlled, or feel like it.

If one or the other or both parties comes into the other's life for a while, this can be tolerated as long as it remains within the threshold of comfort. **If you feel uneasy answering certain questions, you really do not have to! No one is supposed to interfere with your planning—even just daring to say something.** You are fresh, starting a brand-new life, and this gives a fresh energy. Many people, just because of their intrusions and their criticism, would create psychological impediments to your projects and to the way you organize your future. **You are pregnant with a new life. Protect it against any intruders and curious people.**

Light up and ignite your spark alone; never wait for someone to do it for you. Remember: your dreams and your goals are yours only, and whoever comes into your life will always put vetoes, limitations, and constraints on you. There is no other way to live as a couple: you always have to compromise! The problem is that most couples miss a compromising balance in favor of one partner taking more and more room for his or her dreams and comfort. There are even despots and egoists who really need to control their partners totally to feel fulfilled, and they are happy only when the other is annihilated. Think of that and give yourself time—time to reach your own equilibrium without interference. Do not be too eager to come close to your counterpart, be it in good or bad circumstances. Emotional bounds are not so easy to dissolve. But you must do it now, absolutely. Anything else would be detrimental right now.

It is difficult to address men and wives together in my book because there exists indeed differences in the way women and men face and react to problems. We do not want reactions to invade your private and spiritual sphere. That is, you do not want to be put under pressure and explode. There are only a few rules that can prevent it from happening:

1. Living in separate places. Cohabitation while divorcing can become pure horror. You may have seen the film *The War of the Roses* (1989) with Michael Douglas, Kathleen Turner, and Danny DeVito. It is neither normal nor advisable for people who are divorcing and organizing their future accordingly, and who at times become enemies because of their pending disputes before the court, to continue to live under the same roof. Unfortunately this was also my own problem, since my ex-husband left home only when the divorce procedure was at a close. He had long before said he was not interested in living in our flat anymore, and this was the reason why I did not move elsewhere myself and waited for him to leave. A drama! It's absolutely necessary to avoid this. You need an extra reservoir of strength to face the amount of stress triggered by such a situation.

2. Set socially and legally accepted rules on the time your ex spends with the children. Lacking this, one or the other can make continuous claims, come and go at will, and invade the other's private sphere, which is absolutely to be avoided. It is a little different when the ex partners have a wonderful relationship and can talk about weather, bird migration, and dates without starting to insult each other.

3. Talk about hot issues in public places. That is, make appointments at bars or restaurants, or in the park. A strange, open, and crowded background, when needed, will prevent your discussions from going overboard.

4. If you have absolutely **no communication problems** and you have divorced without any pending conflict, there is also no reason to keep your ex at a distance if you both feel that, essentially, you can still enjoy and take advantage of staying friends. You are very lucky if this is your situation. But please be sure that the other party has the same opinion of your relationship. **Some people will never admit that behind their "stay friends" agreement hides the hope of re-winning the love of their ex partner.** Be true to yourself, and should it be necessary, maintain distance (AGAIN)!

5. Limit the number of phone calls by trying to gather together more reasons for calling. Each call can be a serious danger to your tranquility, and neither of you needs more stress.

6. Look at your Vision board with your life goals at least every evening and start working on them. Also, when you think that your life was perfect as it was before divorcing, and you were content like that, you must admit that if it has happened, you were living in a lie and that you deserve true love and true dedication from your partner for life.

7. FAIRNESS, RESPECT, AND RESPONSIBILITY must be reciprocal. Do not expect your partner to be fair if you provoke him or her with impossible requests and pretenses. If you think you are right but receive a very bad reaction, you may consider submitting the argument to your legal advisor or to your best friend in order to understand whether your claims are really just or just egoistic. Responsibility is one of my favorite words because when you have provided for everything you ought to, you feel really satisfied and serene. Staying together involves a number of life projects, changes, and cancellations (regarding career dreams, family dreams, location dreams, etc.). Even more adjustments and compromises have followed the arrival of offspring (if any, as usual). A divorce should not turn into a drama for the weakest parties, and here responsibility plays a big role. I do not want to preach sermons. I think my message is clear enough.

The joy you start to feel deep in your heart, thanks to your new positive attitude, will make every step lighter. It will be also easier to turn your back to people who have done it first. I just erased friends of my ex who did not behave fairly or neutrally. There are a lot of really good people who will be astonished when you tell them that you are divorcing or you have divorced. There are others who have received favors from your ex, and their loyalty makes them particularly funny. I understand. And everyone must also understand that this is a time for making ORDER in your life: clean, lean, simplified, and optimized are your key words. You do not need to put your nerves under further test. You do not need around you people who are not on your team. You can also play alone or with your people. Erase from your address book and ban from Facebook all those who stay there only to spy on what you do, to criticize, or to manipulate or whatever makes you upset. You must not be upset, my dear, you must be HAPPY!

ROSSANA CONDOLEO

HOW TO CHOOSE A GOOD DIVORCE LAWYER AND MANAGE YOUR MEETINGS

The good lawyer is not the man who has an eye to every side and angle of contingency, and qualifies all his qualifications, but who throws himself on your part so heartily, that he can get you out of a scrape.

- Ralph Waldo Emerson (1803 - 1882)

Writer, essayist, philosopher

You have learned that your thoughts shape your life (in different ways). Then why not visualize your ideal attorney for family law—also called a divorce lawyer—the one who will ***get you out of a scrape?*** OK, you are free to give him or her a WOW body and a deep sexy voice as long it can help!

If money *is not* a problem for you, you might be able to engage the best Divorce Lawyer on the market and be prepared to pay a fortune to have things done in the shortest time possible, so that you can continue undisturbed to produce wealth. If money *is* a problem, you might be eligible for free legal advice, performed by state agencies and/or private institutions and legal firms who are engaged in assisting the needy pro bono. Criteria for qualifying may vary from state to state and include a very low income, age, disabilities, military service, being a victim of violence, etc. Be aware that court fees are sometimes included, sometimes to be paid separately from your attorney fees, depending on the state in which you are divorcing. Many differences in laws and regulations make it impossible for me to give you any clue about proceedings, time, and details. Every state, every single county, has its own rules.

When it comes to choosing your divorce lawyer, do not consult the Yellow Pages or the Internet just to pick one with a nice name or a two-page ad. Ask among your people, and the people of your people, if they know someone with proven good performances as a divorce lawyer, that is, a lawyer specializing in family law. Please do not engage any "generalist" or someone with a specialization other than this! The best thing to do is asking people who are used to dealing with family lawyers often; they can tell you who the best is based on their experience —judges, court clerks and employees for example. Carefully read the quote at the beginning of this chapter.

What a Good Divorce Lawyer Must Be Able to Do for You in the First Place

After the first contact, when you are asked to provide detailed information concerning yourself, your ex, your children, your residence, your possessions, and the financial situation of both spouses, every good divorce lawyer must be able to put you at ease, let you calm down (should you be under stress, which is normal for most—even the richest and the most self-confident!) and clearly showcase in- and out-of-court best options and actions to protect your rights and interests, covering (where relevant):

- alimony

- children - support and alimony, time and responsibilities, health insurance

- real estate

- insurance policies

- bank savings, share, stock accounts, and deposits

- pensions

- prenuptial agreements

- Social Security

- health care insurance

- right to maintenance

- inheritances during the marriage

- any other shared possessions and rights (for example, who will keep and take care of the pets).

A good lawyer must be also able to show you facts and uncertainties without letting you hope for or count on (making hazardous and premature forecasts) material possessions that will be subject to dispute with the ex or to court validation. You do not want to plan your future on an uncertain basis. So ask your lawyer again and again whether what he or she says is based on matters of fact or is just an optimistic or pessimistic expectation. This is really very important in order to avoid disillusionment over the outcome of your divorce proceedings. This will prevent you from perceiving as defeats situations that were not meant to be that way from the very beginning. For example: your lawyer tells you that you have the right to a sum of money as alimony for you and your children, and the sum turns to be a lot lower, which requires you to revise all your plans. This can have a great effect on your psychic balance, and you will then have to refer to all my tips to avoid a divorce burnout.

Everybody would obviously think a lawyer earns his living by defending his clients. But this is indeed a very naive belief. It is also not possible to read the thoughts of the person you have in front of you, in order to judge, at first glance, whether he or she is a good lawyer or not. Then, being informed about a lawyer's duty really helps at least to exclude those who are not good.

Lawyers are generally considered an anchor of salvation, whatever the case, and a divorce lawyer can really make a difference in your future lifestyle. They have enormous powers because the law is not always precise or easily circumvented. I cannot tell how it works in the courts because the law is different in every country and in every state. Most of the time, the bulk of the work is paperwork, which is processed in the court's back offices by public clerks, who cannot see anything about your past life as a good husband or dedicated wife, but only what they have in front of their eyes: numbers and forms and financial statements.

Then you would obviously (again) think that a competent, long-lasting, experienced professional would surely *"get you out of the scrape."* Also a naive belief!

A Lawyer Can Work "For" or "Against" You. Discover How!

A lawyer can really make a big difference by deciding whether to work "for" or "against" you. There are also as many types of lawyers as there are types of persons. To list only a few:

❧ The active.

❧ The passive – They will do nothing, or less than needed, and this equals working against you. You are exposed, like a chick in a prairie owned by condors, to the massive attacks of your ex's lawyer.

❧ The money maker - You are their gold mine.

❧ The Mother Teresa of Calcutta – This is a rare, really rare type, I must say. Their mission is to help people protect their rights, and they accept any kind of client, even the underdog.

❧ The part-time lawyer - Some single mothers and fathers or very old lawyers or those who have two jobs, one for the money, such as being a lawyer, and the other because they are very good at it, such as singing, for example. They process your case as routine, even when you are a "very special case" and urgently need a greater amount of work. They really hate complications, and whatever happens is "normal"—that is, nothing you have to worry about. You personally have to pay the consequences of their "lightness of being" though, and these consequences might turn to be serious, both financially and mentally.

❧ The famous VIP lawyer - "Always a winner" is their motto. This is a real *WOW!* lawyer who leaves everyone (court, counterpart, you) totally speechless. They are brilliant and famous, and they want to remain so. If you can afford to engage one, lucky you!

FOR - A lawyer who works for you, stays at your side, embraces your cause, and fights like a bull for you.

AGAINST - A lawyer who works against you, who will just let his or her paralegals take care of the paperwork and will eventually set no particularly convenient separation and divorce conditions for you, so that the counterpart will not react and the divorce case is closed without entering the arena.

AGAINST - Another way of working against you is shooting a good number of unfounded claims to the counterpart (your ex) so that it is natural you go before the court to defend your rights. The divorce proceedings become bulkier and longer and more tiring, and while you go literally mad in the horror of correspondence, meetings, documentations, proofs, and certificates to be provided, you have become an enemy of your ex and your children (if any and living with your ex). Your lawyer cashes more checks from you, apart the court costs, since his work has become enormous (read "inflated"), without having to, and in the end you have gained nothing from his strategy.

AGAINST - Please be open to what I am going to say: A lawyer is a man or a woman, neither a god nor a goddess, with a certain social, cultural, and financial background. A lawyer might work against you due to his or her prejudices. This can mean you receive less-than-fair treatment. This is really bad and difficult to accept, but it's true sometimes, and I am just trying to open your eyes to hidden aspects that you could discover alone, but only after and at cost of disillusionments and great loss of money. You are there and you see and hear, for example, *What says your ex it would be OK for you to receive as alimony?* This happened to me, and I fired my lawyer immediately after—it was not only immoral, but also an offense to my intelligence! Or: *"Why you do not just accept the conditions as they are? What do you need for a living in the end?"* They want to reduce your expectations so that they can reduce their amount of work! Or: *"Never mind; you are young, and you will be able to work and earn your living without the help of your ex."* Same as before. If you are the weaker party, and your ex holds the financial power, clearly tell your attorney that you wish him or her to *"fight for you and not against you,"* and if the attorney does not react, you can withdraw the power of attorney and search for a more honest one.

Some divorce lawyers would rather work for your ex than for you. That might happen when your ex is a V.I.P.; or because he or she works at the ticket office of the Reds or the Giants; or because you are an immigrant; or because the color of your skin is different; or because the lawyer is a man and a little sexist and you are a woman, or vice versa; or because as a child the lawyer hated his or her teachers and you are a teacher; or you have tattoos; or you are not particularly well groomed; or you are overweight and your attorney is a fitness fanatic with three different gym memberships; or because you have beautiful, cat-like green eyes that remind the lawyer of his or her ex; and so on. Only a lot of money on your part can make all their prejudices disappear. Your cat-like green eyes will also become absolutely beautiful.

AGAINST - Exactly like professionals in the medical fields, divorce lawyers have grown a thick skin against every kind of human disgrace. Your story of martyrdom and all its painful implications are irrelevant...or almost irrelevant...or relevant only to the extent that the lawyer deems them to be relevant. In case the lawyer agrees to listen to your story (they are lawyers, they say, neither psychologists nor social workers!), they will do it almost always without real participation. The lawyers, who are allergic to personal stories and see you more as a purse than as a person, can become very nervous and bad tempered while you are making your "bla bla bla", genuinely thinking you have to tell them why you are divorcing. These legal counselors take your money and rarely get things done.

AGAINST - A lot of sympathy might be offered, real or affected, especially when a legal firm has a desperate need of new clients and cannot wait to reel you in. This does not mean your case will be handled by the senior partner who gives his or her name to the firm and has attracted you into that beautiful law office decorated with marble arches and statues of Eros and Psyche. They do not even ask you most of the time, and blooooooob—your folder falls in the hands of the youngest attorney at the firm, who must still decide whether to specialize in family or traffic law. Therefore, if you want to be defended by a particular attorney, you have the right to ask for him or her. If you have an appointment with Senior Mr. or Mrs. Best Lawyer and you are introduced to the youngest associate as above, beg your pardon because you have to go out of the room for a minute, go to desk personnel, and check why you had an appointment with the senior partner and you got another person taking care of your case instead. Whatever the explanation is, you can cancel the meeting and schedule a new one. Please verify whether you'll be charged for the appointment you're canceling, and insist you had an appointment with Senior Mr. or Mrs. Best Lawyer. Then ask whether there is a fee difference because it can make a real difference if you deal directly with a senior partner rather than with a young associate. Control what names are on the power of attorney when you sign.

In reality most of the big ones, the top divorce lawyers, who are also the best paid, have teams of lawyers and students working for them. This makes their results good, since they can assign more people to work at the same case effectively and faster. Then they control the output and appear at meetings and court hearings. This is what everyone would like to have, but it is unfortunately a matter of how much you are available or can afford to pay.

Divorce Online

They claim to work at a distance. And most of the time it is true! It also happens, though, that after you register, they offer to have a legal advisor come and visit you at home. You can deem this a good thing; after all...hey...you can meet your lawyer face to face without having to take a step out of home! It sounds great! Some will accept this without thinking of the consequences. That is: you have to pay for car mileage. Or if they come by public transportation, you must pay for their train, air, or bus tickets, accommodations (if any), and hours lost while traveling to your home. You are not always presented in advance a price list with these extra costs, which will also include an hourly consulting fee. Most of these are hidden costs, so when you sign a service delivery contract (it may be called something else, but it's the document stating you engage them for your divorce), you may have no idea what you are about to pay if you wish to meet your attorney personally. Online divorce has a limited application, which is that it works for those of you who have minimal or no shared interests with their ex-life partners. In complicated divorce cases, meetings are sometimes required (involving the two parties and their respective lawyers) in order to amicably settle disputes concerning possessions, or the children, or both. Internet conferences are also a great possibility for meeting with your online divorce lawyer. In the end, the concept of online consulting is intelligent, convenient, and cheaper; these lawyers don't have to pay big money to keep a physical law firm open, which usually means a nice office in a nice building, with nice front desk personnel.

- Try not to go blind about quality. After identifying one or more suitable names, search online for reviews and entries on major search engines and groups. Gathering information is topical. Reviews might be fake, for example, when they contain no real clue about the people who wrote them, or if they are exaggeratedly positive (which can be true, but go on and look further for confirmations), or they are repeatedly published on more than one web site, group, forum, or whatever.

- Let them show you the price lists, both for online and offline services. If you are sent a contract binding you to buy a "packet" of services in which most are irrelevant to you, then look for something else or for another "packet" with services meeting your special requirements.

- **Pay only through certified payment means**—that is, through those means that give you the possibility to withdraw your payment or receive a refund in case the service is not delivered or only partially delivered.

- **Always make a copy of anything you send via regular mail.** Should you be required to send originals, please ask if an authorized or certified copy is also OK, or make copies and send them by registered mail with return receipt.

- **Control what they do.** Write down any due date (they have to tell you what the deadline is for any procedure) and on expiration, send update requests. This applies also to "physical" lawyers.

How to Increase the Efficiency of Your Divorce Lawyer

You now have a better knowledge of how things go and what you have to know before signing a power of attorney; you can withdraw it later on should you discover that your divorce lawyer is not doing the job properly. This is not advisable, though, because it can cost double the money and cause a great amount of mental stress. Therefore, it is advisable to take more time and make a good choice at first.

You cannot read inside a consultant's head and decide whether he or she is the one. But it can help if you can do something in order to optimize his or her efficiency. You are in a position to positively influence the lawyer's approach to your case, so that he or she will work for you eagerly and effectively. Remember, lawyers are only human beings and sometimes need motivation! So **here is a list of...**

Twenty "Tips and Tricks" for Holding Successful Meetings and Having a Great Relationship with Your Lawyer

1. Prepare at home a list of questions you want to ask, following the criteria you find in the first section of this chapter. This will help you verify whether they will take care of all your interests.

2. Maintain a well-groomed appearance, including clean and neat.

3. Have a self-confident attitude.

4. Smile!

5. Think of all the possibilities that may negatively influence your meetings and try to eliminate them or put a cover on them at the meeting. For example: you are a man with two children who is divorcing his wife because you have discovered you are gay and you like dressing in pink and wearing high heels. Please leave your high heels at home and wear a normal outfit for men if you do not want to risk compromising your meeting and defense due to the lawyer's slight cultural prejudices about homosexuals or transvestites. You may argue: "Better no such a lawyer then!" Then it is OK. Another example: you are divorcing because you want to keep your twenty-three parrots free to fly at home, and your ex does not accept it. Do not bring any of them—your parrots, I mean—to the law firm since your lawyer could be allergic to birds or may judge your conduct a little too "original" for his tastes and **refuse to defend you. Yes, they can refuse you as a client!**

6. Never paint a situation worse than it is. They could feel overwhelmed and unable to help you.

7. Be as concise as possible while telling your story. They do not want to know how many teeth remain in the mouth of your seven-year-old boy.

8. Trust your lawyer and remain trustful as long as he or she deserves it (you now know more about how your lawyer should help you). It is very important that you delegate to your lawyer the problems he or she is trained to handle. And it is important for your lawyer to feel that you trust him or her. This gives him or her motivation.

9. Think of how you can make your lawyer proud of defending you.

10. Always be nice; your lawyer works for you but is not your slave.

11. Have respect for your lawyer's private time and do not call in the middle of the night (should you have obtained his or her private number) or too often. When you are just about to call, think twice about whether this is a good reason or if you can postpone the question to your next meeting. You may be able to summarize many questions in a short e-mail or fax, giving your lawyer time to ponder and answer effectively.

12. Do not think your lawyer can solve your psychological problems. It is very nice when a lawyer is warm and lets you perceive that he or she is there to help. But do not overwhelm him or her with too many problems. You have indeed to tell your lawyer if your ex is abusing you, either physically or mentally, or taking advantage of you financially. You must report this! But the number of times a day you cry thinking of past times does not fall under a lawyer's competence.

13. Let your lawyer inform you about the proceedings.

14. Ask your lawyer to send you copies of reciprocal correspondence and allegations concerning all parties involved, which includes third parties (authorities, institutions, insurance agencies, and so on). This may cost you more money, but you will be constantly updated and know exactly what is happening behind the scenes. On the other hand, almost daily updates on legal issues can generate an unnecessary amount of psychic stress. At times it is really more convenient to let your legal representative take care of your interests and rights and be called to speak for yourself only when it is required. This saves you a lot of mental energy, which you can dedicate to pursuing your goals.

15. Punctually pay your lawyer's fees, if they are fair. Outstanding payments make everybody nervous, and you do not want this to negatively affect your divorce proceedings. On the other hand, if you are waiting to process the payment because you do not understand what you are going to pay, or because the fee is too high for the services you received, **you can resolve your concerns directly with the account office of the law firm or with the attorney in person.** You can do it by telephone or in person at your next meeting; should the answer not be convincing enough, you can go to the BAR Association in your town, county, or state and ask for their opinion and intervention if needed. BAR Associations are lawyers' professional bodies that usually regulate and control, upon request, lawyers' practices in order to ensure high professional standards and fairness to the clients in their districts.

16. Punctually provide your family law consultant with the documentation he or she requires from time to time, so that the divorce machine does not have to stop because of a missing piece of paper. At times you may have to go many years back, to the beginning of your marriage. This is sometimes hard research work because you surely have not preserved documentation of every piece of information you will be asked to deliver. But make your best effort to find them. Unfortunately, sometimes big results depend on small details in the legal field, where almost every word must be "attested."

17. Keep your relationship strictly professional. If your lawyer is a WOW! blonde with the longest legs you have ever seen, keep your hands in their place and forget attempts to get intimate until after your divorce is closed. Any mix of personal feelings in such a relationship can prove to be detrimental, especially if things do not go well.

18. If the lawyer is already a friend of yours, try to keep the private and professional spheres separate. A good friend does not always make a good lawyer.

19. In some countries or states, the spouses are allowed to share the same lawyer, which reduces fees and processing time. But it is not always a good idea, especially when the lawyer in question comes directly from, or on suggestion of the social network of one of the spouses. For example: the attorney plays with your ex-spouse once a week at the golf club! Men especially are able to use their network of friends well. In this case, the friendship of one spouse with one of the two parties **can literally "bring the other party to ruin."** If you want to be sure you are treated equally, have a lawyer for yourself only, or be the one who first engages the lawyer.

20. After your divorce has been decreed, call or write your divorce lawyer every time your ex-spouse will not abide by the law or by the legal agreements that he or she signed, whether it concerns finances, possessions, or children. Be prepared to face the fact that because your marriage is ended, that does not mean that you have not to "bear" your ex-spouse remaining in your life, some way due to the above-mentioned reasons. Avoiding friction will be your first priority, especially when small children are involved. Any problem concerning them should be reported to your divorce lawyer, who will take the necessary steps to pursue and protect the interests of the children before the appropriate authorities. This will cost money: EVERY WORD & ACTION FROM A LAWYER COSTS MONEY!

I really want to close this chapter by wishing you the best divorce lawyer ever. They really make a difference in the quality of your divorce experience. **A good lawyer will take a lot of bad thoughts and concerns away from you**, preventing extreme reactions that are normally due to the feeling that you are left alone and unprotected against duties and preoccupations. They will ensure that your present lifestyle will not be affected by too-radical changes and will work behind the scenes as silently as possible so as not to disturb your life more than it is already.

Once you understand that your attorney is good, you have to relax, trust him or her, and let him or her work for you while you work your way to a happier life.

Happy Divorce!

I really want to close this chapter by wishing you the best divorce lawyer ever. They really make a difference in the quality of your divorce experience. **A good lawyer will take a lot of bad thoughts and concerns away from you**, preventing extreme reactions that are normally due to the feeling that you are left alone and unprotected against duties and preoccupations. They will ensure that your present lifestyle will not be affected by too-radical changes and will work behind the scenes as silently as possible so as not to disturb your life more than it is already.

Once you understand that your attorney is good, you have to relax, trust him or her, and let him or her work for you while you work your way to a happier life.

LOOKING FOR A NEW SPECIAL SOMEONE

Marriage is the triumph of imagination over intelligence. Second marriage is the triumph of hope over experience.

- Samuel Johnson (1709 - 1784)

Writer, essayist, poet, moralist

I do not assume that you are looking for a new husband or wife, or for anybody special at the moment. But the time will come when you are ready to open your heart again. Until that day, no one knocking at your door (how beautiful or rich or both he or she can be) will be interesting and good enough for you, even when you genuinely make attempts in that direction and go out and intermingle with entire crowds of princes or princesses. This is a matter of fact, as researchers have found out. If you have spent many years as *a single in the couple* and you have learned how to cope with love and sex famine and loneliness, sublimating some needs with gardening or any other hobby or profession, or diverting love on humanitarian causes, volunteering, and so on, now you are, so to speak, "stronger" than those who absolutely need a man or a woman to feel they are alive and whole.

There is also no particular need to worry about how long you have being living without sex. If you search the Internet, you will find out that many couples have spent a great part of their marriage without warming their bedroom. In essence, if you do not feel any urge for "physical exchange" and "heart closeness," you do not need to drive yourself in the quest for the Paradise Lost. This does not mean, though, that you must continue breeding beautiful English roses instead of looking for a water bed for you and your new lover! Openness is first of all a state of mind and does not imply any particular action. So please, relax and keep reading.

How Divorce Can Change Your Approach to Love

Divorce proceedings usually trigger two different extreme reactions concerning the way you see the other sex (please read "same sex" if you are gay):

1. You are so worn out and nauseated that you hardly see a possibility that someone can find a place in your bed right now. No, no, no! You are really not thinking about your lingerie or your six-pack now, and you look much more like a bear about to live in its cave until spring than like a blooming bud. Your face gives no room for interpretation: "Closed until unknown date."

It is fear. It is repulsion. You have your head full of preoccupations. Please make your mind free for short periods during the day and think positively of a new feeling—not of a person, but a new feeling that is so filling and sweet that any other feeling takes the backseat. Tell yourself that you want to be thrilled to the point that your skin shivers and your eyes look brilliant. This feeling is love, and in your case you first have to think about love, not about a person in particular. You have to love Love before you can love another man or another woman. You have to crave love because this is the most important premise for you to open your heart to new encounters, or just to realize that the friend who has been helping you in a number of ways since the very beginning of your divorce has been patiently waiting to be noticed. You have to think of being hungry for love because love is a magic wand that turns everything gold—and also your divorce problems, if any. I am talking about love, not the love for your children and your pets and your hobbies, which you may have preserved intact. The love which only a "special someone" can arouse in you, provided you heart is open to receive it. You do not need love; you can cope with everything alone, of course. But love assigns your life another quality no matter how long it inhabits your heart. So please, every night before sleeping, dream about falling in love and smile with joy thinking that maybe tomorrow you will meet that special someone who will give you the key to a special happiness. Love is beauty per se—even when it is not reciprocated. From "one-way love" come thousands of poems and novels. And still it is love. I wish your love to be reciprocated, of course, but I want you to understand what I mean.

2. On the other hand, you can be so desperate for love, so crying for love, because you miss it so much after parting from your ex-spouse, that you may go through several unpleasant experiences before realizing that you have to take into account your past experiences and be responsible about your love relationships at least as much as you are in other areas of your life. Especially if you are a parent, it is of no use for you to bring home a new "special one" every week. Your children might also be desperate for love and could find these experiences very destabilizing.

At first, try to keep your family members a little bit out of your new love life. Bring home only those "special friends" whom you have already given a chance to stay. Until that day, you can date whoever you want if it makes you happy, provided you are aware of what you do. There are many who have gotten married to their schoolmate and never had the opportunity to know other than a single partner in their life. If their divorce is not already the result of a rebellion against this fact, the need to find out, through several encounters, whether they have lost something in their life, can be very strong. For all of you craving love, I hope you can *manifest* the ideal partner in short time. You have answered the Questionnaire at the very beginning and then placed your dreams on your vision board. Focus on your requirements and feel joyful in advance, for you will surely meet the one you want.

Believe in the host of opportunities that now exist, and welcome love when it knocks at your door.

A Matter of Time?

Because it seems you never have enough time to do the things you like, especially now that you have added issues to address and resolve, it would be good if, several times a day, you **repeat this positive affirmation: "I have a lot of time for myself and for finding my soul mate."** This message will reach your subconscious sooner or later, so that in a few days you will be observing that you really have more time and maybe also more occasions for meeting new people. Never give up when you are about to focus something that will positively influence your life. **Only through dedication, feeling, and repetition do affirmations work.**

Internet Dating Survival Guide

The Internet era has produced new ways for people to search for their soul mates, or flirtations, or whatever they deem enticing and appropriate for themselves. This has also produced the **cocooning phenomenon**—i.e., considering home the place for everything from work to digital social life.

The Internet pioneers (I am one of them) once used to define PC activities as *"virtual,"* in opposition to physical interactions, which were defined as *"real."* I am relieved that in the end, it is commonly accepted that PC and the Internet are nothing other than further means of communication (like telephone or fax) and that people behind PCs are as real as their digital interactions. The fact remains, though, that those who want only to exist as "virtual identities" or fakes are also able to do so. These people take advantage of the majority who are good willed and fair, and play with them as if they were playing video games. It seems that a good percentage of relationships, including long-lasting marriages, were born through Internet connections and dating websites. The latter might host fakes who enjoy it if you fall in love with them but never appear to be available to meet you outside the chat room. You never know who hides behind a photo, or whether the real age matches the given age, and so on, until you have made searches yourself or met him or her personally. If you are convinced that this guy or girl is going to make you happy one day, set timelines; after the third time you receive a denial to meet in person, stop your contacts and inform the website owner. Especially when you are a paying member of a dating website, you must expect that people there are not fakes. Make a selection... There are dating websites that manually screen every new member and verify their addresses before putting them online; this requires more personnel and increases their prices. Others leave their members the freedom to abuse the system and offer no real preventive control; these are cheaper or gratis dating services, which pay their bills through advertising. If you really intend to find your date online, take a look at the many independent reviews available on the Internet before signing in.

Before meeting a new online date alone:

~ Verify his or her identity.

- Look for the person's name on major search engines and social networks.

- Check telephone directories.

- Search for the person's address on maps that possibly offer a satellite view of his or her home, where you can match the person's description with the image on your PC.

Your first date should be in a crowded place and should never involve intimate encounters, since you have to be sure this person means what he or she says. We are talking about a special one, not a flirtation; if you are looking for flirting or sex, then OK, but even in this case, try to find a location that leaves your date no possibility of abusing you, should he or she be completely different from the description or arouse no special sexual interest in you. The first time, you must be and remain in a position to leave or ask for help if needed, be it for flirting or sex or a serious relationship.

Divorce *happens*, unfortunately, even to old couples, when the children are grown up and well situated, and some faults in the partner, instead of disappearing, have become even more unbearable after retirement. The much-longed-for and awaited time for living without problems, without having to work and to have more time for fun, turns into a hell. Think about those couples, for example, where one or both have been immersed in their professions and have spent limited time with the family or couple. It is no surprise that certain situations become explosive at a certain time, and even at the age when no one is expected to leave, some leave anyway to get their life back. For these older people, the Internet is really a "magic" way to fill the emptiness left by their ex-partners. Nonetheless, the elderly should also act upon those who want to take advantage of their money and possessions. Younger, attractive hunters especially have the greatest chance of breaking through their natural defenses. There are also a number of dating sites reserved for "young looking for older." Many present their interest in mature people as a genuine need for emotional security, but the security they eventually look for has mostly a material nature. Awareness is the key. If you know that in advance, and you are prepared to pay for it, it is OK. In the end, especially when you are a smart, self-confident, wealthy gentleman or lady, I do not see any reason why you should not use your power of attraction in the love arena. Why not, if it makes you happy and younger? See *Playboy* magazine owner Hugh Hefner or Ivana Trump!

There are members who are 100 percent real and are more than pleased to meet you in person. But some meet in person seven or more love candidates a week. You find them there, year after year after year, always "looking for my soul mate for a long-lasting relationship or marriage." Is it true? Or do they just use this to have date after date after date? Pay attention to the year of registration, the number of stars, or whatever reviews other members have given before. Read again and again the profile and search for reference events in the past. Ask how long he or she has been looking, and if he or she is an old member, think about whether it is appropriate to meet a mighty Old Fox.

Speed Dating and Single-Parent Trips

Almost everybody knows how speed dates are carried out based on the principle that if you do not like someone in the first seven minutes, there is nothing that connects you. Unfortunately, I was unaware of this principle before meeting my ex-husband, whom I gave much longer than seven minutes to root inside my heart, only to find out many years later that we indeed had nothing to share and nothing connecting us. There are contrasting opinions about speed dating. The cost to join a session is generally low, sometimes as little as fifteen dollars, so everyone can try it without spending a fortune. You can find speed dating locations in your area by looking on the Internet. There are a lot of providers. Usually there are not more than ten men and ten women, and there are also gay speed dating services.

You sit in front of a candidate and ask questions. You evaluate him or her based on a form you are given at the very beginning. After seven minutes, a bell rings and you meet another candidate. And so on. At the end, you get the contacts of the people you are interested in and who reciprocate your interest. This step can be made online or directly onsite (depending on the method followed by your speed dating agency or provider).

Interaction between the Internet and speed dating go further: on the Internet you are sometimes given photos and profiles of candidates whom you can invite to appear at the next speed date meeting at the nearest location (usually restaurants at the end of the day or parish halls). You can normally find at least one speed dating location within a 100 Km radius (when not in your same town), so it is really easy to attend such meetings. Opinions are divided: many find this way not only thrilling and time saving (in comparison with online dating sites, where you exchange a number of e-mails and messages before being able to speak face to face), but also effective. Others, who do not report positive impressions, are usually introverted people who really would need more time to get acquainted and give their best; this is the reason why they do not find such short, timed encounters to be fun. In essence, they feel under stress and rarely repeat the experience. I think it is very good to search locally, and speed dating works locally.

It's up to you to go and participate in speed dates taking place very far from your home if you want to add more possibilities to your portfolio.

Then there are agencies that specialize in short travel experiences (normally no longer than one week) for single parents. This is great because apart from singles meeting singles, children play a big part in this because they travel as well. The trips are usually really nice and well organized, and there are trips for all tastes and for all budgets. Of course they include activities designed for children, so they can have fun while you connect with other single parents. If the candidate of your dreams (the one you describe in your Vision board) is not to be found among the travel participants, is not that bad! In the end you have had a nice time with your children and enjoyed the company of people, also of your sex, who know how it is in your situation and can qualify as future friends.

A good, safe way to meet someone is to look for agencies that organize their trips with equal numbers of male and female participants based on age segments (so that you are not at risk of traveling with too many older or younger people). For gays there are also a number of travel agencies, but they are normally oriented to singles without children since there is not enough demand for these cruises among single gay parents. If you find traveling vacation opportunities a good idea, search far in advance (many months before your holidays) so as not to risk running into problems with overbooking.

Are Classic Old Ways OK for You?

Classic old ways to make new acquaintances really do work when you have a consistent friend network locally. For example: "Oh, you know, I have invited my friend David to join us at the after-party; he likes movies and the theater like you!" Or "My sister-in-law is coming to visit us for the weekend, and I was wondering if you could take her out for dinner.... You know, she is young, and...well...with the children, we cannot go out so easily!" If you are new in town, you should want to make new friendships. It all starts with a wish, a dream. Some months after filing for divorce, I understood that my friends network was very much connected to my ex, and not very apt (for the reasons explained in the previous chapters) to make my life easier as a new single. I *genuinely* wished to get to know new people, especially women who were similar to me—that is, strong but not dominant, feminine but not overly sweet, serious but not austere, sparkling, open-minded, positive persons. I had also come to the conclusion that I knew no women at all with my zodiac sign, Capricorn, at least not locally. I must have put all my feelings into thinking and wishing that because only a week later I casually started, in situations in which I was alone (at the theater, for example), to meet new women, most of them separated and divorcing, and most of them Capricorns! I must say that in all my life, I have never gotten to know so many women similar to me in character and of the same sign. And following these new acquaintances and friendships, I started to go out more than before, to have fun again, and to feel less alone. It is no miracle, as explained in the first chapters. It can be the result of various mechanisms that start and end in our mind or that start in our mind, get in touch with the universe, and then come back to us bringing results after results. Then, if you have friends to go out with or to count on, new intriguing acquaintances on the love front will come, sooner or later, especially if you *genuinely* wish to meet your soul mate and so doing make your subconscious mind alert for the target.

Ideally, a person who is looking is accompanied by another person who is looking or is engaged and makes things easier. You are good willed and receptive to love, and you now find more time, but nobody is available to accompany you out: friends and colleagues are all married and do not want to upset their partners going to discos or to clubs; or they think discos and clubs are places of perdition rather than common open places to meet other people. There are cultural differences from state to state, from county to county, from town to village, from friend to friend. Finally, if you really do not find anyone to accompany you out, going out alone is really an option. Start looking around for other divorcing or divorced people at your job or gym. Sign up for new courses (dance, language, do-it-yourself). If you are a parent, look for other single parents while waiting for your child to finish his or her sports lesson. It's time you start thinking positive about encounters. That is, just think you are attracting your ideal candidate, the one with the physical and psychological features you have described in your Vision board. The more you focus on him or her, the more your subconscious will be alerted and send you hints. Sometimes you meet someone who seems interesting, but you are not able to develop any good feelings in this person's direction. Then please, listen to your heart because the first time I did not do it, I gave my ex a second and third and even more chances, which all ended up in a too-long, procrastinated divorce. Do not think that you are "too picky" or that you have to compromise. You have already compromised too long or too much. Now is the time for you to get what you really want, and no one can tell you something different or make you eat a coconut donut if you want a chocolate muffin! This is your life, and you live it according to your own requirements and expectations.

Some Important Dos and Don'ts

You should be allowed to open any door as far as your happiness is concerned, provided you stay ethical and respectful of other people's rights. You can really be creative and imagine and pursue whatever makes you smile just thinking of it. You can do that, or you can have that, if you really want it.

What I am doing from the beginning is providing you with spiritual and practical guidelines in order to become a Happy, Divorced Person. Why? Because happiness is basically a state of mind, but when you do not help, the chances to get it are less. If you keep your expectations high (which you must do!) without sustaining them with positive approaches and practical actions, you might never be in a position to see your dreams come true. Translating the concept into this chapter, for example, it means that if you never leave your home, it is possible that your ideal candidate, the one on your Vision board, will only appear in the form of the milkman, or the postman, or of a driver with a vehicle breakdown. So posting, for example, personals (anonymous or open) in local newspapers and magazines, or contacting a wedding agency could be a good idea. It really depends on where you live, too. If you live in a small village in Alaska and you know by name all the inhabitants, then online dating services might be the best option. **Again, *"help fortune to help you!"***

I know that if you are a father or mother, you would like your children to have a happier parent than you are now. And maybe you are also looking for someone who can support your parenting. Please, always put in your profiles and descriptions that you are the mother or father of one or five or whatever. These are not things you can hide and tell on your tenth date, believing he or she will be so much in love with you that this will represent the least important detail. Not at all! There are people who are strongly against having children. These people are not family oriented and never become so, although they can try, just to do you a favor. So if between your first name and your last name you introduce the fact that you are a single parent, you save a lot of time, disillusionment, and useless quarreling.

On the other hand, there are others who put pictures of their children all over their dating profiles, and it is evident that they, the children, are the center of universe for these people. A more balanced approach would show the person alone, and one image, only one, of his or her children. Otherwise the message to visitors is that a future mate will occupy just a small place in that family.

Back to the Dos and Don'ts, you should not wait until the tenth date to mention chronic and degenerative diseases and serious health problems. The person you are dating has the right to be informed about aspects of your health that could affect his or her own quality of life in the future, should your relationship go as far as marriage. Every nice, good-willed, flexible, and understanding person vacillates when faced with *important late revelations*—i.e., made when one thinks the relationship is strong enough to resist every earthquake. This proves to be completely wrong almost every time: besides their difficulty in absorbing the waves, the other party also starts to question him- or herself about your straightforwardness in general. **No strong fundamentals means no good start, which means no long-lasting relationship.**

Therefore, it is important to balance the flux of information on a first date, but not when it concerns your most important statuses: "I am still married," "I am a single father of four," "I suffer from diabetes," "I am infertile," and so on. It is one thing to keep the conversation light, and another thing to hide major issues. I hope you have cleared up some of these things before you become more serious about your relationship, especially if you have known each other at a distance and he or she must fly thousands miles to come to visit you. You must be true to yourself and to your future partner. I could tell you a number of stories about people I know whose relationships ended very poorly because of **late revelations.**

You know life more than you did when you met your ex-spouse the first time, and yet, depending on your age and situation, you may find yourself a bit rusty concerning flirting and dating in general right now. Well, thousands of people are in the same situation out there! Nobody expects you to have the charm, appearance, and self-confidence of James Bond or Rihanna. I would be very happy if you follow the tips in the chapter about appearance, and after making a little check and improving what there is to be improved, you really do not have to worry about anything else. Just remain true to yourself.

Always ask about your date's job! Men and women alike are always eager to talk about their projects, their colleagues. The topic is really big enough to slip into a number of other subjects. Furthermore, your date will think you are truly interested. Include questions about children (if any) and hobbies.

If you are starting to go out with someone new, keep your dates "light and fresh" (as already hinted); you are not going to tell the whole sticky, muddy story of your divorce, indulging in details and preoccupations that would make a saint run away after the first ten minutes. You are looking for a lover and partner, not for a supernatural rescuer. You will use the positive energy and influx coming from love rather than a direct help in your problems with lawyers at this time. Every overload, every problem that you bring to a fresh new date or relationship might be fatal. You are not going to test your first new date against his or her ability to dry your tears and pay your bills! Please be as independent as possible, both mentally and financially, because the biggest mistake you can make is to base your future on someone else's shoulders. *"Help yourself and Heaven will help you too"* is an ancient Greek saying. Or *"The whole secret of existence is to have no fear. Never fear what will become of you, depend on no one. Only the moment you reject all help are you freed."* - Buddha.

In your forties and over, it is very likely that the singles you meet will be separated or divorced themselves. It is a good idea to forget your problems, if any, and be completely open and focused on your date or brand-new relationship. You are a beautiful blue dragonfly. Enjoy life (again) and be happy because it is what really matters now!

Golden First Date Rules Only for Men

I have tried, and hopefully succeeded, to make my advice gender neutral. But clichés can make life difficult on your first date, when you have to play all your assets. So here are a few golden tips to improve your results.

The majority of women on their first date will be making a 3D portrait of you as a whole (your intellect, body, character, well...yes, sometimes also your equity account and Ferraris). While talking, they are scanning and weighing all the information you give and looking for key features. One of these is **"balance."** Divorced women in particular do not like very much to incur problems involved in "exceeding" resources used in climbing or bodybuilding or running marathons, or whatsoever, which could have been the very cause of their divorce. Men are not always in a position to balance **in-family and out-of-family interests and activities.** Also, my first preoccupation as a freshly divorced lady is to find a settled-down man who has time for our children and me and not only for his friends' network and his hobbies. There is a point when *"understanding"* becomes scarce, and if you are a man and you spend the first forty-five minutes of your first date only talking about your spinning workouts and your spinning weekends, I will spend the remaining two minutes thanking you for the *"nice time"* and explaining to you that although you are a "very interesting person" (which is a terrible lie), unfortunately it has not clicked and I wish no more contacts with you. This is really a pity if you are not the type who spends all his time practicing indoor bicycling but are timid, not very talkative, and you have chosen this topic thinking that girls love sports-enthusiast guys. It is the same for any other activity or hobby that is extremely time-consuming. I know men who spend all of their free time inside their cellars putting together model airplane kits. What the family does up there, in the ground-floor living room or garden, is not their business. Also on the weekends, they fly away together with their model airplanes to gatherings at private airports, locally, nationally, and abroad. So unless you meet an airplane model fan, I would discourage you from talking about your hobby, and also from practicing it so exclusively. If you love model airplanes so much, you might want a housekeeper rather than a love partner or a new wife. Of course, this discussion of airplanes is only an example.

Women like generous men. It has always been so and it will be so in the future, regardless of role divisions or financial possibilities. When you go out of the restaurant where you had your first date paying only for your meals and you also ask who has to leave the tip, well...NO GO. The girl or lady in front of you can also be Ivana Trump in person and submerge you with gold, but the fact remains that women like polite men and they will forgo politeness only if the man can abundantly compensate this lack with a number of other qualities. Then, if you are good looking like Denzel Washington, intelligent like Einstein, and funny like Jim Carrey, you can eventually pay separate bills at the restaurant. I hope it is clear.

Stating your firm belief that the prenuptial agreement is a warranty for getting "pure love" on your first date can also be lethal. Honest, but lethal!

Women do not like to wait too long. Most men think that "taking it slow" is what women want. FALSE! You will fail to catch your butterfly in the net if you are distracted and slow. Whenever you have a special interest for a special woman, you had better make it clear—and fast. Ladies in their thirties and over react restlessly to slow flirting; they finally fly away to look for other colorful and promising flowers. Let me say that a too-fast approach is a lot better than a too-slow one. So: think, think, think.

If you tell her "I will phone you" after you have said good-bye, PLEASE DO IT! Women are known to hover over the phone for hours, days, weeks, before they eventually understand that you will never dial their number in a lifetime. So make no promises. Just say "Good-bye." Nothing is compulsory after a good evening spent together except good manners—even when, with a deeper glance into her décolleté, you discover that the pink lady in pink is filling her bra with toilet paper (not even those spongy lift supports they use to enhance their breast size!). Disillusionment is common, especially if you have met your date on the Internet and she has Photoshopped all of her pictures.

A good gentleman remains a good gentleman, and after you pay the restaurant bill and if she is indeed your butterfly, propose something to do right afterward (coffee, music club). If she doesn't accept, extend an invitation for an all-day date. You will have more time to get to know each other.

Please understand that this is not a dating guide (maybe I will write one; stay tuned!) and that I have to make all my readers happy, even those who already have a special one and have not bought this book for this sort of advice. So I'll stop here, although the topic is vast and really interesting.

Golden First Date Rules Only for Women

As I've already written for the men, I have tried, and hopefully succeeded, to make my advice gender neutral. But clichés make life difficult on your first date, when you have to play all your assets. So here are a few golden tips to improve your results.

The man you have been waiting for is late? It does not mean he's going to stand you up. He's just late! Please do not get nervous on your first date because of frivolous reasons. For example, your hair is sitting on your forehead and does not want to go back in place; the flu has left a bit of hoarseness and you feel more a frog than a princess; you have got your cycle...God, this is really a problem, em...this is, well...sure, this is a sign you should not rush into more than allowed on a first date! Yes, it is important that you look good and that you are natural.

Men do not like too much makeup or too many colors (unless you want only to flirt). If you leave more than half your legs naked under your skirt, then he will think you want an "all you can eat" first date. Are you sure is this the message?

He sits there, in front of you, and he says nothing—because you have been talking all the time! Please ask questions about his work and his favorite hobby, and wait...and wait. Silences are very nice too. You can understand a lot of things from how a person masters silences on a date. There can be room for a lot of eye contact.

It is absolutely a no-go that you tell him to give up something (from his smoking habit to his favorite hobby) on your first date ("It is not healthy to smoke," or "What the heck? Free climbing can be really dangerous. You'd better play golf instead," etc.). Men react as if under high voltage to any kind of constraints. You are adults who have had past lives, and if he is divorced, he is enjoying his life more than ever—no one is limiting him now! So if you do not come to terms with his hobbies and smoking habits or whatever, you had better let him go rather than test his ability to adapt to your wishes.

Everyone is a world, and I cannot generalize; I do not know you, and you are free to say and do whatever you think appropriate on your date. But another mistake that we women very often make is playing the companion role. I am one of these, for example. I have a very male side in me, and I tend to be a bud most of the time. I like this camaraderie with men, and it is so good to have their friendship, but you are not going out with that guy because you want to be his friend. Are you? There is nothing more demoralizing for men with erotic intentions than a woman who can tell him how he feels under his pants. You are a woman, and he is a man. And you are on your first date. Your understanding of men's world is good? Terrific! Cool! Nice! But do not tell him how he should look and smile at the WOW blonde drinking two seats over. This is suicide. If you are interested, do not send false messages of non-interest. Do not test in this way or in a similar way whether he is interested. Most guys are not tuned to Radio Psychic. They think straight and simple, so do the same and you will win their heart!

I have already written about what is likely to make your date run away through the men's room window of the restaurant where you go for your first date. Let me spend a couple of words more, from girl to girl. Pssst, nearer. Well they, guys, are usually threatened like lambs followed by wolves when you ask: "Are you planning to marry again?" Or should he be a virgin single (read not divorced), "Is marriage somewhere in your future plans?" Unfortunately, even in the event the man is well intentioned to marry sooner or later—and maybe he is dating you because he finally wants to settle down (again)—this is a question that raises his wild, atavistic fears and switches his red alarm mode on. You can be nice, intelligent, interesting, sexy, and cute, and have natural D cups, but he will always see you as the wolf that wants to eat him. No go!

I would like to go on with this topic, and perhaps I will write a dedicated book, but I cannot make this chapter bigger. There are readers who already have someone special at their sides and must skip over pages about love affairs.

I wish that you will soon find your perfect soul mate!

GOOD LUCK!

HOW TO HELP YOUR CHILDREN THROUGH DIVORCE

Nothing has a stronger influence psychologically on their environment and especially on their children than the unlived life of the parent.

- Carl Gustav Jung (1875 - 1961)

Psychoanalyst, psychiatrist, physician

I really do not want to say too much about this subject; the terrain is very sensitive. I strongly support what Jung said, and for those who had no life in the marriage, then it is good that they look for fulfillment. **There is no worse parent than an unhappy parent.**

Children mostly suffer in silence, and you see how their feelings change while trying to adapt to new situations. Their faces are strangely sad as soon as divorce becomes an issue in the family. It's terrible!

I am the mother of a young daughter, and she was proud of her mom-dad-child family. She used to say the word *family* more often than average for children of her age. I guess she took this religious family feeling and a special love for traditions partly from me. And then, in her eyes, at the beginning, I was the one to blame for dismantling her beautiful family vision. She could not know that filing for divorce was a pure necessity, the *only way left* for me to escape from the grave of my marriage. How many parents feel guilty? Ninety-five percent at least. Well, do not do it! Your children will understand later. Give them time, and they will understand your motives.

A Short Meditation and a Meaningful Affirmation for You and Your Children

Before going further, I want you to take a couple of minutes to meditate, to empty your mind of anything contingent.

~ SHORT WHITE MEDITATION ~

Sit down and breathe deeply.

Relax and focus on WHITE.

Let the color of pureness calm you and help you forget problems and confusion.

Do not control your thoughts; your inner peace will take care of them.

Focus on white light and feel how happy you become while this light enters your body and makes it luminescent.

You are now the source of light.

Your peace and your light pervade everything in your surroundings.

~ * ~

Now repeat the following three times:

~ AFFIRMATION ~

I am just going through a particular time of my life, and this will be soon over.

I provide my children with love, tenderness, care, and affection, and I am available to understand their special needs.

My children are happy, I am happy, and we enjoy the life we want.

I am happy, my children are happy, and we enjoy the life we want.

~ * ~

You might want to practice my short combination of meditation and affirmation when you feel insecure or a little bit down, or at any time you want. It makes you stronger and stronger. You are a light for your children, a guide for their lives. But happiness is a right of yours and the necessary base for further development.

This affirmation is not in conflict with the advice I gave you in the first part, <u>which sounded more or less like</u>: ***"Be more selfish and care less about other people's issues right now..."*** in order to save precious life energy for yourself at this time—energy to be loving, understanding, and supporting.

Another thing is pandering to their every whim. For example: *"Dad/Mom, I want to eat ten ice creams today. Can I?"* *"Yes, of course you can!"* Or: *"Dad/Mom, could you please do my homework for me today?"* *"My dear, consider it done!"* and so on. These are erroneous ways to support your children through and after divorce. You would quickly go mad: you are no longer a good parent if you let stress get you down. A Dad or Mom on the brink of burnout is no ideal parent. You do not want to go insane because your load of duties has tripled (divorce problems, your normal daily duties, the extra duties generated by your children), do you? No, no, no!

If you are the other parent who sees the children on weekends, it is workable for a certain time. Your children's conversations with their schoolmates might sound like this: *"You should have your parents divorce so that you get double ice creams, double presents, and double holidays, like me! I can help you develop a strategy to break them up."* I do not find a deep educational message in what the *compensating* parents try to do. The words *too much* really do not apply as far as love, understanding, and engagement are concerned. On the other hand, compensation through material things would bring them to think that everything in life can be repaired and obtained through money (which is partly true—grin!), and they will repeat this model with their special ones. There is a great chance you are also a child of divorce, and you learned this model from your parents. If so, it is time to break the chain and start on a new course. Let's see how.

It was a long way to get up to here, but you have learned that:

Divorce is a fact, not a state of mind. The state of mind you develop in connection with it is yours, and you can change it so that if your marriage had no happy end, at least your divorce will, and this is a certainty if you follow my advice. No one knows better than I do how mind-consuming divorcing can be. But we have both learned that focusing on the positive sides of a fact can turn advantageous, not merely positive. Once upon a time there was a family with an unhappy dad and mom. **<u>Let's see how it looks like in your children's eyes and what would they say:</u>**

Old Negative Family Situation:

1. *I am in a dad-mom-children family configuration.*

2. *Dad and Mom are depressed/quarrel/are nervous/do not talk to each other/are unhappy/are absent.*

3. *I get love, but more love would be better. It seems they are just not focused enough on me lately, due to the problems they have with each other!*

4. *I would like them to stop talking nonsense to each other that way! I cannot stand them anymore. I wish they would get divorced, so that this "cats and dogs" situation would go to an end.*

5. *I do not like to see my dad and mom so unhappy. I really feel uncomfortable. Furthermore, I cannot do much about this situation.*

6. *And now please stop, you two! I have to do my homework, and my life is totally upside*

down. I just want a bit of normality, and no more insanity at home!

7. (If you have become addicted or seriously depressed due to your marriage problems, you might be unable to carry out your normal daily duties at home and for your children. Then it is possible...) I no longer want to be called Stinky! And I am just fed up with eating hot dogs and pizza every day. Please give me a normal dad and mom who care about me!

New Positive Divorce Situation:

1. I am in a one-at-a-time parent-child family for the moment (who knows, I hope I will be in a patchwork family soon—more people, more fun!). I spend more time now with my dad/mom than ever before. And we do a lot of interesting things together. When I go out with Dad, Mom has time for herself, and vice versa, so that they can do what they like most.

2. They are happy now—my parents, I mean— and they can even talk to each other without biting. That's great!

3. *4, 5, 6, 7. Wow, they are so balanced now that they have much more love to give me! They smile. And it is as if the sun is shining again at home. Everything is clean, and I have a different breakfast every day. I really do not know how my dad/mom takes so much time for me. But it is simply great! Divorce was the best thing they could have done—for us all! Yes, and I get the best notes at school again. Well, I now understand that a "normal" family can only be so when all the people in it are content and at peace with one another. I am young, but I also understand that you must be happy with your partner; otherwise it's better to be single and looking for a new partner. Anyway, we are always a family! A happy family!*

~ * ~

Now, I simplified the situation to remind you that, basically, it's behind you—that is, the past. Divorce is a great possibility not only for you, but also for your children, to regain balance and live happier and realized.

Twelve Very Important Rules to Make your Children Happy Through and After Divorce

1. GOLDEN RULE: Talk to your children and explain what is going to happen. They must not ignore your plans to divorce when a final decision has been made. Ideally, both parents should agree on what to say, gather the children, and then tell them. Use simple words, even if they are already grown-up teenagers. Leave details out (for example, *"I caught your father by surprise sleeping with a brunette wearing red stockings and a push-up bra from Victoria's Secret's 2012 collection."* No graveyard tones; maintain positive outlooks. It should be more or less short and simple: *"Dad/Mom and I are not happy together. You might have realized it. We have tried to settle our conflicts, but unfortunately, it doesn't work! Therefore, we will divorce. This means that your dad/mom and I will no longer live together. This has nothing to do with you. We are both super happy parents and really fortunate to have you as children. We will be able to be better parents* *for you than before because the time we used to spend in conflict will now be used to make us happy. The only difference is that Dad/Mom is going to live somewhere else, and you will be visiting each other during the week or on alternating weekends (or whatever). This will bring more interesting things in your life and more opportunities to learn and to have fun. We want you to share with us your thoughts anytime."*

If you already know about important changes (address, town, job, state, etc.), you can tell them now and then ask whether they have questions. Otherwise you can inform them (see below) whenever changes occur that may interfere with their present life and for which they have to be informed and prepared in advance. Don't tell them about minor changes—those that do not affect their habits—don't charge the children with too much information. Try to ensure that their everyday life runs as normal as before, before conflicts and problems. Prepare them slowly for changes so that changes (I repeat) do not happen abruptly.

2. Do not allow yourself feelings of guilt. You simply do not have to, as already pointed out. You have learned how many possibilities are waiting for you, how life will be pregnant with anything you desire. And if you wish and engage, nothing can stop you from attaining your goals. You can provide your children with your love, care, and support as usual and even more, and the other parent will be doing the same (hopefully). If divorce is not the result of a caprice, you really do not need to feel guilty.

3. YOU are divorcing, not your children, nor your family (your father, mother, siblings, etc.). As sad as it can be, even in the worst circumstances, when you ex-partner has behaved like a monster, a vampire, unless otherwise set forth by the court, he or she remains a parent to your children, although in another form (depending on the custody). You cannot expect your family to hate your ex the way you do, or to estrange your ex as you do. And this is especially true for your children.

4. If it is not easy to say something good about your ex-partner to your children, talk about him/her as little as you can. Do not traumatize them with loads of adult concerns (especially if they are still small children). Some bad spouses can become even worse ex-partners during and after divorce, particularly about financial agreements and child maintenance. And if they are not so generous, why should you care that your children maintain a good idea of the other parent if he or she behaves like a jackass? Well, you do not have to! Your children are able to judge for themselves, based on their own experience. Good surprises are not excluded! A lot of people become better parents after divorcing; their sense of responsibility and attachment to the children can eventually grow.

5. Do not expect your children (both small and adult) **to help you in any crisis or during emotionally stark moments of your divorce process.** Please avoid transmitting your insecurities (if any) to them and cope with problems alone. Also, grown-up children might react dramatically to changes in the configuration they have left at home. Adult children of divorcing or divorced parents feel responsible for the happiness of their parents, and this can bring nervousness in their own family lives. Before you relieve and lighten your heart by pouring your troubles on them over and over, be sure that they are not struggling themselves against difficulties at home; what if they are facing financial or work drawbacks, or they are experiencing a problematic relationship at this time? They might not be strong enough to accept or undertake extra emotional stress and become depressed, since their pillars (their parents) have fallen down. Marriage problems should never be the subject of parent-child talks, at any age. Tell them only what is strictly necessary to explain—why you have made the decision. Do not bring despair into their lives. Friends and marriage or divorce counselors usually do a better job. If you need a new home, you can go and stay with your adult children for a little while, until you have found a suitable home (the sooner, the better). But please consider that they have their own life and their own family, and your presence can disturb their social and inner balance. Again, your stay should be strictly limited to the time you need to find a new permanent accommodation.

6. Be sympathetic. When I see clouds in her eyes, I always ask my daughter: *"Are you happy?"* Listen what they say, and give them the positive certainties you have at hand. Do not promise them that the world shall remain the same if it is not so. It is also apparent: changes are in the air! And they must know what happens and be involved in the process. When looking for a new home, for example, or other things that affect their private spheres as well (new school, new dance course, etc.), they should be asked about and able to actively participate in the choices you make. This turns unwanted changes into thrilling new experiences.

7. Children are adaptable, but... Children of divorce usually understand better the mechanisms that regulate relationships, and in comparison with children of *non-divorced parents*, they are indeed more adult. Which is not always a bad thing! Every child or young person, though, reacts differently. Some of your children could turn out to be more sensitive than others. Try to understand if they need a special approach. If you have problems in addressing the topic alone, you might call the family council in your county, or other public or private institutions and agencies that provide family counseling both in ordinary and special situations.

8. Look for help. Divorced parents who remain the sole caregivers of children with chronic diseases need special aid and support. If this is your case, you might qualify to receive free social services. Before changing your work habits, in order to stay at home more to assist your care-needing children, find out what is available locally, including voluntary associations and foundations, to help you take care of your special child.

9. Help your children maintain their relationships with grandparents, relatives, friends, and other connections they have on the other parental side. If a change of residence is required, they can still keep their connections via Skype, e-mail, and Facebook, and by visiting. It is important they feel that their world is not going to disappear, but only change a little.

10. Let go of hurt. Ephesians 4:31 ESV: *"Let all bitterness and wrath and anger and clamor and slander be put away from you, along with all malice."* I know it is very, very bad. You might feel (because of your divorce) betrayed, lonely, groundless, financially insecure, worthless, awful (if ex has disappeared with a younger and beautiful lover), annoyed (you have lost your central seat at the opera and the access card to the Gold Club); socially frustrated (people no longer bow while saying hello since you are no longer the wife of the Japanese Emperor), etc. Hey, let's stop here! I have not been writing advice till now to come to the end and still hear that you are in a life crisis. So please, REWIND! You no longer have such problems because you focus on:

- **your life**
- **your goals**
- **your feelings**
- **your future**

ﻌ **your job**

ﻌ **your finances**

ﻌ **your relationship to your children.**

YOUR EX IS PAST AND YOU ARE A BRAND-NEW PERSON, A HDP (even if you are still in the process of divorcing). The wished-for developments in your private, social, and job departments are starting to appear, and your attitude and mood are already much more positive than they were before you started to read my guide. I can feel that! You are enlightened by the awareness that not only will your life work without your ex, but it will work one hundred times better than ever before. And as far as your relationship with your children is concerned, you can regain ground anytime and be a better parent than ever.

10. Stay connected to your children, physically and mentally. Spread love all over. Kiss them. Hug them. Tell them "*I love you*" every day, and many times a day. This is the best way to assure them continuity and groundedness. Also in those cases in which a divorce brings a change in status (which financially and practically means that everything becomes a little less and a little smaller), this is only a temporary situation. You have the power to provide them again with all the comforts they are used to living with. In any case, children are not attached to "things" the way we are. You had better ask, and always ask your children what they deem important, since sometimes we really worry for nonexistent reasons! *"Mom, mom, mom…!"* said my daughter while pointing her small finger at me. *"Why did you buy so many pieces of clothing? I really do not need them all! I need only a couple of them!"* My reaction was not that of a mother proud of her mature little child. Not at all! I felt a rush of genuine anger. And a lot too! I had paid quite a lot of money for that Internet order! I had spent more than a couple of hours on my tablet PC while on our summer vacation to provide her with nice clothes for the school year (fall and winter). And then she was pointing her finger at me as if it were nonsense and I was wasting money. I had expected something like *"Oh, mom, you angel, how wonderful! I like everything you bought for me!"* Well, I must admit it: that was an MCA (Material Compensation Attack), one of those I was previously speaking out against! My daughter simply reacted so wisely! She was only five! Surprisingly adult and poised! Back to that moment: I stood there completely astounded. I thought she would cry for joy at seeing all those new, appealing things scattered all over in her pink room (my aim was to make a nice surprise). No need to further clarify the concept. Connect to your children and try to give them what they need, not what you think they need. Well, my daughter underestimated her actual needs; I had not bought anything superfluous, in my opinion—in the end.

11. Learn new parenting skills. If you or the other parent cannot make a boiled egg or give an aspirin in case of fever, the problem should be addressed before the children get used to pizza or Emergency and Rescue Services. Anyone who is willing to be a good parent will also make some small efforts in that direction. Adding new competencies and skills in your *parenting service* is morally A MUST when your EX spouse is no longer there to help. On the other hand, if you or your ex has enough money to hire a nanny, why not? Provided the nanny does not also take care of all the children's homework and free time.

12. Avoid promiscuity. In the previous chapter I pointed out how important it is to be serious about inviting new partners home. You could argue that your children have a dad and a mom, and when anyone comes to visit and stay for the night, it is your private thing and no one, not even your children, has the right to interfere. I find this concept disputable, though.

The home where you live is also their home. The new partners you bring home are new human elements in their lives, in that an acquaintance process starts in their mind. Smaller children get used to the idea that those people might cover a paternal or maternal role, especially when they have no regular contacts with their other parent. On the other hand, sometimes the acquaintance process runs not so smoothly and generates rejection and conflicts ("He is not my dad!" or "She is not my mother!"), which can be very hard on the children until they finally accept them as your new partners. These internal adjusting processes are not void of serious psychological problems if the new partners you bring home change again and again and again. Without limiting the number and variety of your flirtations and partners, which is really your business, you could still respect the harmonious and balanced lifestyle of your children by just enjoying this number and variety of partnerships outside your home. And do this until you have found someone special so that you can proudly announce: *"Hello, children, this is Tarzan/Jane. He/She is my new partner."* Promiscuity should never be a solution, particularly when you really feel alone and you are looking for love and not sex. It is different if this lifestyle is the product of your choice and not a desperate quest for reciprocated love. Children judge and neither forgive nor forget! Morality can represent a solid standing pillar in the life of a family where the ground has become unstable due to divorce complications.

Anyway, I often paint a situation darker than it is at first, aiming to make you more sensitive and aware of facts and their consequences. **Reality can be a lot easier and lighter, especially when you have started to think like a Happy, Divorced Person—someone who has dreams and pursues them with joy.**

From deep inside my heart, I wish you...

...Happy Divorce!

ROSSANA CONDOLEO

- 316 -

ABOUT THE AUTHOR

Eclectic Forward Thinker, International Writer and Life-Coach dedicated to Helping People live a Happy and more Fulfilled Life.

Rossana Condoleo provides counselling and coaching services on:

RELATIONSHIP ISSUES: Love & Partnership, Family & Parenting, Separation & Divorce;

PERSONAL DEVELOPMENT AND IMPROVEMENT: Stress Control, Inner Balance, Appearance, Self-Confidence, Leadership, Setting Goals, Motivation.

www.rossanacondoleo.com

Printed in Great Britain
by Amazon

85150792R00181